BETTY CROCKER'S
BREADS

**Golden Press/New York**
Western Publishing Company, Inc.
Racine, Wisconsin

Director of Photography: George Ancona
Illustrator: Malcolm Spooner

First Printing, 1974

Copyright © 1974 by General Mills, Inc., Minneapolis, Minnesota. All rights reserved. No portion of this book may be reprinted or reproduced in any form or any manner without the written permission of the publishers, except by a reviewer who wishes to quote brief passages in connection with a review. Printed in the U.S.A. by Western Publishing Company, Inc. Published by Golden Press, New York, New York.

Library of Congress Catalog Card Number: 74-79002

Contents

Dear Bread Baker,

Welcome—to the warm, comfortable world of homemade breads. For some of you it will be a step backward in time—to the traditional bakings of your grandparents or to *their* grandparents. For others, it will be a step forward, beyond the old and into the new. New shapes and tastes, new textures and techniques. Whatever your approach, bread is still a warm satisfying food that offers much in the making.

Every recipe has been thoroughly tested, first in the Betty Crocker kitchens and then again by home bakers throughout the country. To help first-time yeast bakers, we have summed up the important basic information in the last chapter, and we suggest it as the place to begin. Once familiar with the fundamentals, you will find our collection of recipes for breads, rolls, coffee cakes and even holiday bakings easy to follow.

Whether you bake bread to express your creativity or to bring joy to others, or simply because it's fun to do and tastes so good . . . whatever your reasons, these recipes are for you. Enjoy them!

Cordially,

Betty Crocker

The Bread Board

Slice into your favorite loaf—we've got them all: traditional favorites, ethnic breads, whole-grain loaves. Warm and yeasty and deliciously hearty, part of the modern trend toward old-fashioned goodness. Any wonder that bread baking is back in the home?

Traditional White Bread

The perfect start for an adventure into yeast baking—our best-foot-forward white bread recipe. These snowy loaves signal their fragrant goodness while they're still in the oven.

    2 packages active dry yeast
    ½ cup warm water (105 to 115°)
    1¾ cups warm water
    3 tablespoons sugar
    1 tablespoon salt
    2 tablespoons shortening
    6 to 7 cups all-purpose* or
        unbleached flour
        Butter or margarine, softened

Dissolve yeast in ½ cup warm water in large mixing bowl. Stir in 1¾ cups warm water, the sugar, salt, shortening and 3½ cups of the flour. Beat until smooth. Stir in enough remaining flour to make dough easy to handle.

Turn dough onto lightly floured surface; knead until smooth and elastic, about 10 minutes. Place in greased bowl; turn greased side up. Cover; let rise in warm place until double, about 1 hour. (Dough is ready if an indentation remains when touched.)

Punch down dough; divide in half. Flatten each half with hands or rolling pin into a rectangle, 18x9 inches. Fold crosswise into thirds, overlapping the 2 sides. Roll dough tightly toward you, beginning at one of the open ends. Press with thumbs to seal after each turn. Pinch edge firmly to seal. With side of hand, press each end to seal; fold ends under.

Place loaves seam sides down in 2 greased loaf pans, 9x5x3 or 8½x4½x2½ inches. Brush lightly with butter. Let rise until double, about 1 hour.

Heat oven to 425°. Place loaves on low rack so that tops of pans are in center of oven. Pans should not touch each other or sides of oven. Bake until loaves are deep golden brown and sound hollow when tapped, 25 to 30 minutes. Remove from pans. Brush with butter; cool on wire rack.

2 loaves.

*If using self-rising flour, omit salt.

Variations

Cinnamon-Raisin Bread With the second addition of flour, stir in 1 cup raisins. Mix ¼ cup sugar and 2 teaspoons cinnamon. After rolling dough into rectangles, sprinkle each with 1 tablespoon water and half of the sugar mixture.

Herb Bread Stir in 2 teaspoons caraway seed, ½ teaspoon sage and ½ teaspoon nutmeg before the last addition of flour.

Raisin Bread With the second addition of flour, stir in 1 cup raisins.

One-Rise Buttermilk Bread

2 packages active dry yeast
¾ cup warm water (105 to 115°)
1¼ cups buttermilk
4½ to 5 cups all-purpose* or
   unbleached flour
¼ cup shortening
2 tablespoons sugar
2 teaspoons baking powder
2 teaspoons salt
   Butter or margarine, softened

Dissolve yeast in warm water in large mixer bowl. Add buttermilk, 2½ cups of the flour, the shortening, sugar, baking powder and salt. Blend ½ minute on low speed, scraping bowl constantly. Beat 2 minutes on medium speed. Stir in *just* enough remaining flour to make dough soft and slightly sticky.

Turn dough onto generously floured surface; knead 5 minutes or about 200 turns. Flatten dough with hands or rolling pin into rectangle, 18x9 inches. Fold crosswise into thirds, overlapping the 2 sides. Roll dough tightly toward you, beginning at one of the open ends. Press with thumbs to seal after each turn. Pinch edge firmly to seal. With side of hand, press each end to seal; fold ends under.

Place loaf seam side down in greased loaf pan, 9x5x3 inches. Brush lightly with butter. Cover; let rise in warm place until double, about 1 hour. (Dough in center should be about 2 inches above pan.)

Heat oven to 425°. Place loaf on low rack so that top of pan is in center of oven. Bake until loaf sounds hollow when tapped, 30 to 35 minutes. Remove from pan. Brush with butter; cool on wire rack.

1 loaf.

*If using self-rising flour, omit baking powder and salt.

Note: To prepare 2 small loaves, divide dough in half after kneading and shape as directed. Place loaves in 2 greased loaf pans, 8½x4½x2½ inches. Bake as directed.

To prepare 2 large loaves, double all ingredients except yeast. Blend 1 minute on low speed, scraping bowl constantly. Beat 4 minutes on medium speed. Stir in *just* enough remaining flour to make dough soft and slightly sticky. Divide dough in half; knead each half 5 minutes. Continue as directed.

Variation

Little Loaves After kneading, divide dough into 8 equal parts. Flatten each part into a rectangle, 10x5 inches. Shape as directed. Place in 8 greased individual loaf pans, 4½x2¾x1¼ inches. Bake 20 to 25 minutes.

8 loaves.

Honey–Whole Wheat Bread

Smooth honey sweetness, whole wheat crunchiness. Flavor and texture that recall an earlier time, when home-baked bread was a way of life. Bring a touch of nostalgia into your kitchen with this updated approach to old-fashioned flavor.

---

    2 packages active dry yeast
    ½ cup warm water (105 to 115°)
    ⅓ cup honey
    1 tablespoon salt
    ¼ cup shortening
    1¾ cups warm water
    3 cups stone-ground whole
        wheat or graham flour
    3 to 4 cups all-purpose* or
        unbleached flour
        Butter or margarine,
        softened

Dissolve yeast in ½ cup warm water in large mixing bowl. Stir in honey, salt, shortening, 1¾ cups warm water and the whole wheat flour. Beat until smooth. Stir in enough of the all-purpose flour to make dough easy to handle.

Turn dough onto lightly floured surface; knead until smooth and elastic, about 10 minutes. Place in greased bowl; turn greased side up. Cover; let rise in warm place until double, about 1 hour. (Dough is ready if an indentation remains when touched.)

Punch down dough; divide in half. Flatten each half with hands or rolling pin into a rectangle, 18x9 inches. Fold crosswise into thirds, overlapping the 2 sides. Roll dough tightly toward you, beginning at one of the open ends. Press with thumbs to seal after each turn. Pinch edge firmly to seal. With side of hand, press each end to seal; fold ends under.

Place loaves seam sides down in 2 greased loaf pans, 9x5x3 or 8½x4½x2½ inches. Brush lightly with butter; sprinkle with whole wheat flour or crushed rolled oats if you like. Let rise until double, about 1 hour.

Heat oven to 375°. Place loaves on low rack so that tops of pans are in center of oven. Bake until loaves are deep golden brown and sound hollow when tapped, 40 to 45 minutes. Remove from pans; cool on wire rack. (Pictured on the front cover.)

2 loaves.

*If using self-rising flour, decrease salt to 1 teaspoon.

Cracked Wheat Bread

  1 cup milk, scalded
  ¼ cup molasses
  2 teaspoons salt
  1 tablespoon shortening
  1 cup cracked wheat
  2 packages active dry yeast
  ½ cup warm water (105 to 115°)
  1 cup stone-ground
     whole wheat flour
2¾ to 3 cups all-purpose* or
     unbleached flour
     Butter or margarine,
     softened
     Cracked wheat

Combine milk, molasses, salt, shortening and 1 cup cracked wheat in large mixer bowl. Cool to lukewarm.

Dissolve yeast in warm water. Add yeast, whole wheat flour and 1 cup of the all-purpose flour to the cracked wheat mixture. Beat 2 minutes on medium speed, scraping bowl frequently. Stir in enough remaining flour to make dough easy to handle.

Turn dough onto lightly floured surface; knead until smooth and elastic, about 10 minutes. Place in greased bowl; turn greased side up. Cover; let rise in warm place until double, about 1 hour. (Dough is ready if an indentation remains when touched.)

Punch down dough. Shape into round loaf; place in greased 9-inch pie pan. Brush lightly with butter; sprinkle with cracked wheat. Let rise until double, 50 to 60 minutes.

Heat oven to 400°. Bake until loaf sounds hollow when tapped, 30 to 35 minutes. Remove from pan; cool on wire rack.

1 loaf.

*If using self-rising flour, omit salt.

Variation

Mushroom Bread Decrease cracked wheat to ½ cup and add 1 envelope (about 2 ounces) mushroom soup mix to the cracked wheat. Grease inside and 2 inches of top outside edge of two 1-pound shortening cans. After punching down, divide in half. Knead each half gently until smooth and shape into a cylinder to fit can; press in can. Brush with butter; sprinkle with cracked wheat. Let rise 1 hour. Bake on lowest rack of oven. (Pictured on page 11.)

2 loaves.

Mushroom Bread

Country Oatmeal Bread

Crunchy-sweet oats and robust molasses combine in a loaf that's double delicious for breakfast toast, lunch box, snack time . . . anytime. Slice thin for sandwiches or spread with cream cheese for a snack.

¾ cup boiling water
½ cup uncooked rolled oats or quick rolled oats
3 tablespoons shortening
¼ cup light molasses
2 teaspoons salt
1 package active dry yeast
¼ cup warm water (105 to 115°)
1 egg
2¾ cups all-purpose* or unbleached flour
1 egg white, slightly beaten
¼ cup uncooked rolled oats or quick rolled oats
¼ teaspoon salt

Combine boiling water, ½ cup oats, the shortening, molasses and 2 teaspoons salt in large mixer bowl. Cool to lukewarm.

Dissolve yeast in warm water. Add yeast, 1 egg and 1½ cups of the flour to the oats mixture. Beat 2 minutes on medium speed, scraping bowl frequently. Stir in remaining flour until smooth.

Turn batter into greased 2-pound coffee can; smooth and pat top. Brush top with beaten egg white. Crush ¼ cup oats with ¼ teaspoon salt; sprinkle over top of loaf. Cover; let rise in warm place until double, about 1½ hours.

Heat oven to 375°. Bake until loaf is brown and sounds hollow when tapped, 50 to 55 minutes. (If loaf is browning too quickly, cover with aluminum foil for the last 15 minutes of baking.) Remove from pan; cool on wire rack. (Pictured on page 11.)

1 loaf.

*If using self-rising flour, omit 2 teaspoons salt.

Variation

Anadama Country Bread Substitute ½ cup yellow cornmeal for the ½ cup oats; omit beaten egg white, ¼ cup oats and ¼ teaspoon salt. Smooth and pat batter in greased 8- or 9-inch pie pan, mounding center higher than edge. Let rise and bake as directed.

Breakfast Loaf Substitute ¼ cup light corn syrup for the ¼ cup light molasses. Turn batter into greased loaf pan, 9x5x3 inches. Brush top with beaten egg white; sprinkle with mixture of ¼ cup oats, crushed, and 2 tablespoons brown sugar.

Pictured on page 11: Goodness Bread (page 14), Mushroom Bread (page 9), Country Oatmeal Bread (page 10), Gold Nugget Bread (page 15).

Pictured on page 12: Dark Pumpernickel Bread (page 17), Pioneer Bread (page 13).

Pioneer Bread

1 package active dry yeast
¾ cup warm water (105 to 115°)
3 tablespoons sugar
2 teaspoons salt
1 egg
3 tablespoons shortening
⅓ cup yellow cornmeal
2 to 2½ cups all-purpose* or
  unbleached flour
  Butter or margarine, softened
  Cornmeal

Dissolve yeast in warm water in large mixer bowl. Add sugar, salt, egg, shortening, ⅓ cup cornmeal and 1 cup of the flour. Blend ½ minute on low speed, scraping bowl constantly. Beat 2 minutes on medium speed, scraping bowl occasionally. Stir in enough remaining flour to make dough easy to handle.

Turn dough onto lightly floured surface; knead until smooth and elastic, about 5 minutes. Place in greased bowl; turn greased side up. Cover; let rise in warm place until double, 1 to 1½ hours. (Dough is ready if an indentation remains when touched.)

Punch down dough. Flatten dough with hands or rolling pin into rectangle, 18x9 inches. Fold crosswise into thirds, overlapping the 2 sides. Roll dough tightly toward you, beginning at one of the open ends. Press with thumbs to seal after each turn. Pinch edge firmly to seal. With side of hand, press each end to seal; fold ends under.

Place loaf seam side down in greased loaf pan, 9x5x3 or 8½x4½x2½ inches. Brush lightly with butter; sprinkle with cornmeal. Let rise until double, 50 to 60 minutes.

Heat oven to 400°. Bake until loaf sounds hollow when tapped, 25 to 30 minutes. Remove from pan; cool on wire rack. (Pictured on page 12.)

1 loaf.

*If using self-rising flour, omit salt.

Variation

Pioneer Rolls   After first rising, divide dough into 16 equal parts. Shape each part into a smooth ball, tucking edge under so it resembles a mushroom cap. Place in greased muffin cups or 2 inches apart on greased baking sheet. Let rise 30 to 40 minutes. Bake 15 minutes.

16 rolls.

Goodness Bread

What's in a name? When the name is "Goodness," that says it all. There's the extra goodness of whole wheat, wheat germ and brewer's yeast—and the natural goodness of honey, soy flour and sea salt . . . all deliciously combined in this hearty whole-grain bread.

2½ cups boiling water
1 cup uncooked quick rolled oats
¾ cup nonfat dry milk
½ cup soy flour
¼ cup wheat germ
¼ cup brown sugar (packed)
¼ cup honey
1 tablespoon plus 1 teaspoon sea salt
3 tablespoons salad oil
2 tablespoons brewers' yeast
2 packages active dry yeast
½ cup warm water (105 to 115°)
5½ to 6 cups stone-ground whole wheat flour
Salad oil
Wheat germ

Combine boiling water, oats, dry milk, soy flour, ¼ cup wheat germ, the sugar, honey, salt, 3 tablespoons oil and the brewers' yeast in large mixer bowl. Cool to lukewarm.

Dissolve active dry yeast in warm water. Add yeast and 2½ cups of the whole wheat flour to the oats mixture. Beat 2 minutes on medium speed, scraping bowl frequently. Stir in enough remaining flour to make dough easy to handle.

Turn dough onto lightly floured surface; knead until smooth and elastic, 10 to 12 minutes. Place in greased bowl; turn greased side up. Cover; let rise in warm place until double, about 1½ hours. (Dough is ready if an indentation remains when touched.)

Punch down dough; divide in half. Flatten each half with hands or rolling pin into a rectangle, 18x9 inches. Fold crosswise into thirds, overlapping the 2 sides. Roll dough tightly toward you, beginning at one of the open ends. Press with thumbs to seal after each turn. Pinch edge firmly to seal. With side of hand, press each end to seal; fold ends under.

Place loaves seam sides down in 2 greased loaf pans, 9x5x3 or 8½x4½x2½ inches. Brush tops lightly with oil; sprinkle with wheat germ. Let rise until double, about 1 hour.

Heat oven to 375°. Bake until loaves sound hollow when tapped, 40 to 45 minutes. (If loaves are browning too quickly, cover with aluminum foil for the last 15 minutes of baking.) Remove from pans; cool on wire rack. Cut into thin slices to serve. (Pictured on page 11.)

2 loaves.

Gold Nugget Bread

A round of applause for this round of whole wheat goodness, flecked with shredded carrot and studded with raisins. Good taste, good nutrition and good looks . . . And it freezes for long-term storage. What more could anyone ask for?

    1 package active dry yeast
    ¼ cup warm water (105 to 115°)
    ⅔ cup lukewarm milk (scalded, then cooled)
    2 tablespoons honey
    2 tablespoons shortening
    1½ teaspoons salt
    ½ cup finely shredded carrot
    ½ cup raisins
    2 cups stone-ground whole wheat flour
    ¾ to 1 cup all-purpose* or unbleached flour

Dissolve yeast in warm water in large mixing bowl. Stir in milk, honey, shortening, salt, carrot, raisins and whole wheat flour. Beat until smooth. Stir in enough all-purpose flour to make dough easy to handle.

Turn dough onto lightly floured surface; knead until smooth and elastic, about 10 minutes. Place in greased bowl; turn greased side up. Cover; let rise in warm place until double, 1½ to 2 hours. (Dough is ready if an indentation remains when touched.)

Punch down dough; squeeze firmly to release air bubbles. Shape into round loaf; place on greased baking sheet or in greased 9-inch pie pan. Let rise until double, 45 to 60 minutes.

Heat oven to 350°. Bake 30 minutes. Remove from pan; cool on wire rack. Store in refrigerator after the first day; freeze for long-term storage. (Pictured on page 11.)

1 loaf.

*Do not use self-rising flour in this recipe.

Natural Grains and Flours

Rediscovering these natural flours of yesterday is one of today's delights:

Whole wheat (or graham)—made from the entire wheat berry after it has been thoroughly cleaned.

Cracked wheat—prepared by cracking or cutting cleaned wheat into angular fragments.

Rye—milled from rye grain; usually mixed with wheat for bread baking.

Buckwheat—robust favorite for pancakes; known by its "speckles."

Soy flour—ground from whole raw soy beans; slightly sweet-tasting.

Cornmeal (ground corn) and *Rolled Oats* (oat groats pressed between rollers)—give crunchy sweetness to breads.

Wheat germ—the germinating portion of the wheat kernel.

Swedish Limpa

In Sweden it wouldn't be Christmas without the traditional round loaves of *Vörtlimpor*. But any day's a holiday with the intriguing flavor of this special rye bread. (You'll be glad the recipe makes two loaves!)

    2 packages active dry yeast
 1½ cups warm water (105 to 115°)
  ¼ cup molasses
  ⅓ cup sugar
    1 tablespoon salt
    2 tablespoons shortening
      Grated peel of 1 to 2 oranges
      or 1 teaspoon anise seed
      (optional)
2½ cups medium rye flour
2¼ to 2¾ cups all-purpose* or
      unbleached flour
      Cornmeal

Dissolve yeast in warm water in large mixing bowl. Stir in molasses, sugar, salt, shortening, orange peel and rye flour. Beat until smooth. Stir in enough all-purpose flour to make dough easy to handle (dough will be sticky).

Turn dough onto lightly floured surface. Cover; let rest 10 to 15 minutes. Knead until smooth and elastic, about 5 minutes. Place in greased bowl; turn greased side up. Cover; let rise in warm place until double, about 1 hour. (Dough is ready if an indentation remains when touched.)

Punch down dough; round up and let rise until double, about 40 minutes.

Grease baking sheet; sprinkle with cornmeal. Punch down dough; divide in half. Shape each half into a round, slightly flat loaf. Place loaves in opposite corners of baking sheet. Let rise 1 hour.

Heat oven to 375°. Bake until loaves sound hollow when tapped, 30 to 35 minutes. Remove from baking sheet; cool on wire rack.

2 loaves.

*If using self-rising flour, omit salt.

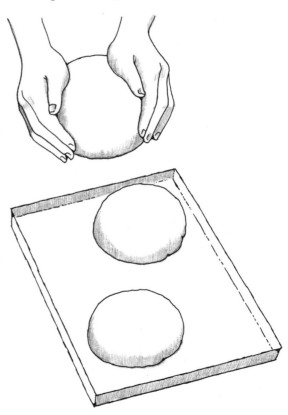

Dark Pumpernickel Bread

Legend has it this moist, deep-brown bread originated in fifteenth-century Germany —the creation of a baker named Nichol Pumper. Now it can serve to enhance your baking reputation, too.

      3 packages active dry yeast
   1½ cups warm water (105 to 115°)
      ½ cup dark molasses
      1 tablespoon plus 1 teaspoon salt
      2 tablespoons caraway seed
      2 tablespoons shortening
   2¾ cups rye flour
      ¼ cup cocoa
   2½ to 3 cups all-purpose* or
         unbleached flour
         Cornmeal

Dissolve yeast in warm water in large mixing bowl. Stir in molasses, salt, caraway seed, shortening, rye flour and cocoa. Beat until smooth. Stir in enough all-purpose flour to make dough easy to handle.

Turn dough onto lightly floured surface. Cover; let rest 10 to 15 minutes. Knead until smooth, 5 to 10 minutes. Place in greased bowl; turn greased side up. Cover; let rise in warm place until double, about 1 hour. (Dough is ready if an indentation remains when touched.)

Punch down dough; round up and let rise until double, about 40 minutes.

Grease baking sheet; sprinkle with cornmeal. Punch down dough; divide in half. Shape each half into a round, slightly flat loaf.

Place loaves in opposite corners of baking sheet. Let rise 1 hour.

Heat oven to 375°. Bake until loaves sound hollow when tapped, 30 to 35 minutes. Remove from baking sheet; cool on wire rack. (Pictured on page 12.)

2 loaves.

*If using self-rising flour, omit salt.

Variations

Light Pumpernickel Bread Substitute light molasses for the dark molasses, omit cocoa and increase all-purpose flour to 2¾ to 3¼ cups.

Pumpernickel Rolls After second rising, divide dough into 12 equal parts. Shape parts into balls or ovals. Place on greased baking sheet. Let rise 40 minutes. Bake until rolls are brown, 30 to 35 minutes.

1 dozen rolls.

Pizza

The pleasures of pizza are as endless as the topping possibilities you can dream up. But first the crust, where all good pizzas begin. And this one's just right.

Sauce (right)
1 package active dry yeast
1 cup warm water (105 to 115°)
1 teaspoon sugar
1 teaspoon salt
3 tablespoons salad oil
3 to 3½ cups all-purpose* or unbleached flour
2 tablespoons salad oil
Toppings (right)

Prepare Sauce. Dissolve yeast in warm water in large mixing bowl. Stir in sugar, salt, 3 tablespoons oil and 2 cups of the flour. Beat until smooth. Stir in enough remaining flour to make dough easy to handle.

Turn dough onto lightly floured surface; knead until smooth, about 5 minutes. Place in greased bowl; turn greased side up. Cover; let rise in warm place 45 minutes. (Dough is ready if an indentation remains when touched.)

Heat oven to 400°. Grease 2 jelly roll pans, 15½x10½x1 inch, with 2 tablespoons oil. Punch down dough; divide in half. Roll each half into a rectangle, 16x11 inches. Place rectangle in each pan.

Spread ½ cup Sauce over each pizza; cover each with one or more of the Toppings. If using more than one, arrange meat over Sauce, then mushrooms or olives; sprinkle cheese over top. Bake 25 minutes.

2 pizzas.

*If using self-rising flour, omit salt.

Sauce
1 can (6 ounces) tomato paste
½ cup water
1 teaspoon salt
1 teaspoon oregano
¼ teaspoon garlic or onion powder
⅛ teaspoon pepper

Mix all ingredients; let stand 1 hour.

Toppings (Use 1 or more for each pizza)
½ pound ground beef, browned and drained
1 pound bulk Italian sausage, browned and drained
2 ounces sliced pepperoni (½ cup)
½ cup sliced mushrooms (4 ounces)
¼ cup sliced pitted olives
1 cup shredded Cheddar or mozzarella cheese (about 4 ounces)

Pocket Bread

Crispy outside, a puffy pocket inside, this Middle Eastern bread starts out flat and "explodes" in the oven. Great for parties: Put out chicken or egg salad along with our tasty meat filling and let guests "make their own."

1 package active dry yeast
1⅓ cups warm water (105 to 115°)
1 teaspoon salt
¼ teaspoon sugar
1 tablespoon salad oil or olive oil
3 to 3½ cups all-purpose* or
    unbleached flour
    Cornmeal
    Meat Filling (right)

Dissolve yeast in warm water in large mixing bowl. Stir in salt, sugar, oil and 1½ cups of the flour. Beat until smooth. Stir in enough remaining flour to make dough easy to handle.

Turn dough onto lightly floured surface; knead until smooth and elastic, about 10 minutes. Place in greased bowl; turn greased side up. Cover; let rise in warm place until double, about 1 hour. (Dough is ready if an indentation remains when touched.)

Punch down dough; divide into 6 equal parts. Shape into balls. Let rise 30 minutes.

Sprinkle 3 ungreased baking sheets with cornmeal. Roll each ball into a circle ⅛ inch thick. Place 2 circles in opposite corners of each baking sheet. Let rise 30 minutes.

Heat oven to 500°. Bake until loaves are puffed and light brown, about 10 minutes. Tear in half crosswise and fill each half with ½ cup Meat Filling; serve immediately or place hot unfilled bread in plastic bags to keep moist and pliable until ready to serve. (Pictured on page 25.)

6 servings.

*Do not use self-rising flour in this recipe.

Note: To freeze, wrap cooled unfilled bread in aluminum foil and freeze. Reheat foil-wrapped bread in 375° oven until hot, 10 to 15 minutes.

Meat Filling

2 tablespoons salad oil
½ cup pine nuts
1½ cups finely chopped onion
2 pounds ground lamb or
    ground beef
2 medium tomatoes, peeled,
    seeded and finely chopped
½ cup finely chopped green pepper
⅓ cup snipped parsley
⅓ cup fresh lemon juice
3 tablespoons red wine vinegar
1½ teaspoons salt
¾ teaspoon allspice
½ teaspoon cayenne red pepper
    Dash of pepper

Heat oil in large skillet over medium heat. Add pine nuts and onion; cook and stir until pine nuts are brown and onion is tender. Add lamb; cook and stir until brown. Drain off fat. Stir in remaining ingredients. Cook uncovered over low heat until liquid is absorbed.

Brunch Bread

½ pound bacon, cut into 1-inch
    pieces
    Salad oil
1 package active dry yeast
¼ cup warm water (105 to 115°)
¼ cup lukewarm milk (scalded,
    then cooled)
1½ teaspoons sugar
1 teaspoon salt
3 eggs
2¾ cups all-purpose* or
    unbleached flour
½ cup diced Swiss or natural
    American cheese

Fry bacon until crisp. Drain, reserving bacon fat. Add enough salad oil to fat to measure ½ cup. Set bacon and fat-oil mixture aside.

Dissolve yeast in warm water in large mixer bowl. Add milk, sugar, salt, reserved fat-oil mixture, the eggs and 1½ cups of the flour. Beat 10 minutes on medium speed. Stir in remaining flour with spoon until smooth. Cover; let rise in warm place until double, about 1 hour.

Punch down batter; gently work in cheese and reserved fried bacon until well distributed. Shape into ball; place in greased 8- or 9-inch pie pan or 9- or 10-inch ovenproof skillet. Let rise until double, about 1 hour.

Heat oven to 375°. Bake 30 minutes. Remove from skillet; cool on wire rack.

1 loaf.

*If using self-rising flour, omit salt.

Sourdough Bread

Sourdough, named for its unique flavor, won its fame in gold rush days, when every prospector carried his own pot of starter. Ours, while less authentic, is more reliable—and it still provides an adventure in old-time baking.

1 cup Sourdough Starter (facing page)
2½ cups unbleached or all-purpose*
    flour
2 cups warm water (105 to 115°)
4 to 4½ cups unbleached
    or all-purpose* flour
1 teaspoon salt
3 tablespoons sugar
¼ teaspoon baking soda
3 tablespoons salad oil
    Cold water

Mix Sourdough Starter, 2½ cups flour and 2 cups warm water in large glass mixing bowl with wooden spoon until smooth. Cover; let stand in warm, draft-free place 8 hours.

Remove 1 cup of the mixture; store in refrigerator or add to any starter you may already have.

Add 4 cups of the flour, the salt, sugar, soda and oil to remaining mixture in bowl. Stir with wooden spoon until smooth and flour is completely absorbed. (Dough should be just firm enough to gather into a ball.) If necessary, gradually add remaining ½ cup flour, stirring until all flour is absorbed.

Turn dough onto heavily floured surface; knead until smooth and elastic, about 10 minutes. Place in greased bowl ; turn greased side up. Cover; let rise in warm place until double, about 2½ hours. (Dough is ready if an indentation remains when touched.)

Punch down dough; divide in half. Shape each half into a round, slightly flat loaf. Do not tear dough by pulling. Place loaves in opposite corners of greased baking sheet. Make three ¼-inch slashes in each loaf. Let rise in warm place until double, about 1 hour.

Heat oven to 375°. Brush loaves with cold water. Place in middle of oven. Bake until loaves sound hollow when tapped, about 50 minutes, brushing occasionally with water. Remove from baking sheet; cool on wire racks.

2 loaves.

*Do not use self-rising flour in this recipe.

Sourdough Starter
    1 package active dry yeast
    3 cups warm water (105 to 115°)
    3½ cups unbleached or all-purpose*
        flour

Dissolve yeast in warm water in large glass mixing bowl. Gradually stir in flour. Beat until smooth. Cover with towel or cheesecloth; let stand in warm, draft-free place (80 to 85°) until starter begins to ferment, about 24 hours (bubbles will appear on surface of starter). If starter has not begun fermentation after 24 hours, discard and begin again.

If fermentation has begun, stir well; cover tightly with plastic wrap and return to warm place. Let stand until foamy, 2 to 3 days.

When starter has become foamy, stir well; pour into 2-quart crock or glass jar with tight-fitting cover. Store in refrigerator. When a clear liquid has risen to top, starter is ready to use. Stir before using.

Starter can be stored for several weeks. If it is not used regularly every week, add 1 teaspoon sugar and stir well. If used regularly, starter will be active indefinitely.

About 4 cups starter.

*Do not use self-rising flour in this recipe.

Sourdough Success Tips

Start bread at night to bake in the morning—or vice versa.

Refrigerated starter should come to room temperature before using.

Keep the temperature as uniform as possible (80 to 85°) to give the starter yeast every chance to grow.

You can vary the amount of baking soda, depending on how sour you like your bread.

Don't "kill" leftover starter by adding anything but flour, sugar and water.

And do note: Although your homemade sourdough will be crisp, tangy and delicious, a home oven cannot duplicate the special hard crust of a San Francisco bakery loaf.

Mock Sourdough Bread

No need for a starter in this updated version of sourdough . . . yogurt gives it a somewhat similar zesty tang. Shy about using too much "sour"? Opt for the lesser amount of yogurt in the recipe. Loaves are shaped individually, so to each his own. Nice for a buffet, too!

2 cartons (8 ounces each) unflavored
    yogurt (2 cups) or 1 carton
    (8 ounces) unflavored yogurt (1 cup)
    plus ½ cup milk
1 package active dry yeast
¼ cup warm water (105 to 115°)
1 tablespoon sugar
2 teaspoons salt
1 tablespoon salad oil
3¾ to 4¼ cups all-purpose* or
    unbleached flour
    Cold water
    Coarsely ground black pepper
    (optional)

Heat yogurt *just* to lukewarm. (If using yogurt plus milk, heat yogurt and milk *just* to lukewarm.) Dissolve yeast in warm water in large mixing bowl. Stir in yogurt, sugar, salt, oil and 2 cups of the flour. Beat until smooth. Stir in enough remaining flour to make dough easy to handle.

Turn dough onto lightly floured surface; knead until smooth and elastic, about 5 minutes. Place in greased bowl; turn greased side up. Cover; let rise in warm place until double, about 1 hour. (Dough is ready if an indentation remains when touched.)

Punch down dough; divide into 8 equal parts. Flatten each part with hands or rolling pin into a rectangle, 6x4 inches. Roll up, beginning at one of the long sides. Pinch edge of dough firmly into roll to seal. With side of hand, press each end to seal; fold ends under.

Place loaves seam sides down on greased baking sheet. Brush tops lightly with cold water. With sharp knife, cut 3 diagonal slashes across top of each loaf. Let rise until double, about 25 minutes.

Heat oven to 375°. Brush loaves with cold water. Sprinkle pepper into slashes. Bake until loaves sound hollow when tapped, 30 to 35 minutes, brushing with water every 10 minutes. Remove from baking sheet; cool on wire rack.

8 loaves.

*If using self-rising flour, omit salt.

Challah Braid

This glisteny golden braid traditionally ushers in the Jewish Sabbath; let it start off any one of your days. A touch of sugar provides just a hint of sweetness that makes this rich yellow bread delicious.

  1 package active dry yeast
  ¼ cup warm water (105 to 115°)
  ½ cup lukewarm water
  1 tablespoon sugar
  1 teaspoon salt
  1 egg
  1 tablespoon shortening
  2½ to 2¾ cups all-purpose*
      or unbleached flour
      Shortening
  1 egg yolk
  2 tablespoons cold water

Dissolve yeast in warm water in large mixing bowl. Stir in lukewarm water, sugar, salt, 1 egg, 1 tablespoon shortening and 1¼ cups of the flour. Beat until smooth. Stir in enough remaining flour to make dough easy to handle.

Turn dough onto lightly floured surface; knead until smooth and elastic, about 5 minutes. Place in greased bowl; turn greased side up. Cover; let rise in warm place until double, 1½ to 2 hours. (Dough is ready if an indentation remains when touched.)

Punch down dough; divide into 3 equal parts. Roll each part into a rope 14 inches long. Place ropes close together on lightly greased baking sheet. Braid ropes gently and loosely.

Do not stretch. Pinch ends to fasten; tuck under securely. Brush with shortening. Let rise until double, 40 to 50 minutes.

Heat oven to 375°. Beat egg yolk and cold water slightly; brush over braid. Place on oven rack below center of oven. Bake until braid sounds hollow when tapped, 25 to 30 minutes. (If braid is browning too quickly, cover loosely with aluminum foil.) (Pictured on page 26.)

1 braid.

*If using self-rising flour, omit salt.

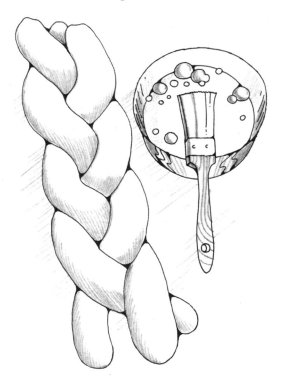

French Bread

A long, slender loaf with a cracklingly crisp crust—as close as you can come to French bakeshop bread. Versatile, too, for sophisticated French toast, hero sandwiches or to "mop up" your sauces in style.

 1 package active dry yeast
1¼ cups warm water (105 to 115°)
1½ teaspoons salt
 1 tablespoon shortening
3½ to 4 cups all-purpose* or
    unbleached flour
 1 tablespoon cornmeal
    Cold water
 1 egg white
 2 tablespoons cold water

Dissolve yeast in warm water in large mixing bowl. Stir in salt, shortening and 1½ cups of the flour. Beat with spoon until smooth. Stir in enough remaining flour (first with spoon, then by hand) to make dough easy to handle.

Turn dough onto lightly floured surface; knead until smooth and elastic, about 5 minutes. Place in greased bowl; turn greased side up. Cover with damp cloth; let rise in warm place until double, 1½ to 2 hours. (Dough is ready if an indentation remains when touched.)

Punch down dough; round up and let rise until almost double, about 45 minutes. Punch down; cover and let rest 15 minutes.

Lightly grease baking sheet; sprinkle with cornmeal. Roll dough into rectangle, 15x10 inches. Roll up tightly, beginning at one of the long sides. Pinch edge to seal. Roll gently back and forth to taper ends.

Place loaf on baking sheet. Make ¼-inch slashes across loaf at 2-inch intervals or make 1 slash lengthwise. Brush top of loaf with cold water. Let rise uncovered about 1½ hours. Brush with cold water.

Heat oven to 375°. Bake 20 minutes. Beat egg white and 2 tablespoons cold water slightly; brush over loaf. Bake 25 minutes longer. Remove from baking sheet; cool on wire rack.

1 loaf.

*Do not use self-rising flour in this recipe.

Variation

Submarine Loaves Divide dough into four equal parts. Roll each part into a rectangle, 6x5 inches. Roll up, beginning at one of the long sides. Pinch edge to seal. Make one ¼-inch slash lengthwise down each loaf. Let rise uncovered until double, about 40 minutes. Bake about 15 minutes. (Pictured on page 25.)

4 loaves.

Pictured on page 25: Submarine Loaves (page 24), Pocket Bread with Meat Filling (page 19).

Pictured on page 26: Challah Braid (page 23), Brioche (page 27).

Brioche

1 package active dry yeast
½ cup warm water (105 to 115°)
2 tablespoons sugar
½ teaspoon salt
5 eggs
1 egg, separated
¾ cup butter or margarine, softened
3½ cups all-purpose* or
    unbleached flour
1 tablespoon sugar

Dissolve yeast in warm water in large mixer bowl. Add 2 tablespoons sugar, the salt, 5 eggs, the egg yolk, butter and 2 cups of the flour. Blend ½ minute on low speed, scraping bowl constantly. Beat 10 minutes on medium speed, scraping bowl occasionally. Stir in remaining flour until smooth. Scrape batter from side of bowl. Cover with plastic wrap; let rise in warm place until double, about 1 hour.

Stir down batter by beating about 25 strokes. Cover bowl tightly with plastic wrap; refrigerate at least 8 hours.

Stir down batter. (Batter is soft and sticky.) Divide into 4 equal parts. Shape 1 part into ball on lightly floured surface. Shape remaining batter into one 6-inch flattened round.

Grease 9-cup brioche pan, 3 to 4 inches high. Place large round in pan, patting to fit. Make indentation about 2 inches in diameter in center; place smaller ball in this indentation. Let rise until batter is 1 inch from top of pan, about 2 hours.

Heat oven to 375°. Beat egg white and 1 tablespoon sugar slightly; brush over small ball only. Do not let egg white mixture accumulate around edge of pan. Bake 1 hour. Immediately remove from pan. (Pictured on page 26.)

1 brioche.

*Do not use self-rising flour in this recipe.

Variation

Individual Brioches Grease well 24 medium muffin cups. Divide chilled batter in half; refrigerate one half. Shape remaining half into roll about 7½ inches long. Cut into 15 slices, about ½ inch thick.

Working quickly with floured hands (batter is soft and sticky), shape 12 of the slices into balls; place in muffin cups. Flatten and make a deep indentation in center of each. Cut each of the remaining 3 slices into 4 equal parts. Shape each part into a small ball; place a ball in each indentation. Repeat with remaining half of batter. Let rise until double, about 40 minutes.

Heat oven to 375°. Beat egg white and 1 tablespoon sugar slightly; brush over small balls only. Do not let egg white mixture run down into muffin cups. Bake 15 to 20 minutes. Immediately remove from pans.

2 dozen individual brioches.

Onion Turbans

2 packages active dry yeast
2 cups warm water (105 to 115°)
1 envelope (about 1½ ounces)
    onion soup mix
¼ cup sugar
2 tablespoons molasses
1 teaspoon salt
1 egg
⅓ cup shortening
6 to 6½ cups all-purpose* or
    unbleached flour
    Butter or margarine, softened

Dissolve yeast in warm water in large mixer bowl. Add soup mix; stir to dissolve. Add sugar, molasses, salt, egg, shortening and 3 cups of the flour. Beat ½ minute on low speed, scraping bowl constantly. Beat 2 minutes on medium speed, scraping bowl occasionally. Stir in enough remaining flour to make dough easy to handle.

Turn dough onto lightly floured surface; knead until smooth and elastic, about 10 minutes. Place in greased bowl; turn greased side up. Cover; let rise in warm place until double, about 1 hour. (Dough is ready if an indentation remains when touched.)

Punch down dough; divide in half. Roll each half into a rectangle, 24x5 inches. Roll up, beginning at one of the long sides. Stretch and shape until even. Beginning at outside edge of pan, coil roll seam side down in greased 8-inch pie pan or round layer pan, 8x1½ inches. Brush coil generously with butter. Let rise until double, about 50 minutes.

Heat oven to 375°. Bake until turbans are golden brown, 25 to 30 minutes. Cool on wire rack.

2 turbans.

*If using self-rising flour, omit salt.

Variation

Onion Braids Divide each half of dough into 3 equal parts; roll each part into a rope 14 inches long. Place 3 ropes at a time close together on greased baking sheet. Braid ropes loosely and gently. Pinch ends to fasten; tuck under securely. Brush lightly with butter. Let rise and bake as directed.

2 braids.

A Roll Sampler

When is a roll not a roll? When it's a French croissant, Italian breadstick, English muffin, German pretzel. In this chapter are great traditionals such as these plus up-to-the-minute dinner roll recipes, too. Why not try your hand and sample them all?

Traditional Dinner Roll Dough

The shape's the thing! From a basic dough you can enjoy a different roll every night of the week. And hot rolls have a way of making even the simplest of meals say, "I care."

- 1 package active dry yeast
- ¼ cup warm water (105 to 115°)
- ¾ cup lukewarm milk (scalded, then cooled)
- ¼ cup sugar
- 1 teaspoon salt
- 1 egg
- ¼ cup shortening or butter or margarine, softened
- 3½ to 3¾ cups all-purpose* or unbleached flour
  Butter or margarine, softened

Dissolve yeast in warm water in large mixing bowl. Stir in milk, sugar, salt, egg, shortening and 2 cups of the flour. Beat until smooth. Stir in enough remaining flour to make dough easy to handle.

Turn dough onto lightly floured surface; knead until smooth and elastic, about 5 minutes. Place in greased bowl; turn greased side up. Cover; let rise in warm place until double, 1½ to 2 hours. (Dough is ready if an indentation remains when touched.)

Punch down dough. Shape any of the following rolls. Let rise 20 minutes. Heat oven to 400°. Bake until rolls are golden brown, 15 to 20 minutes.

*If using self-rising flour, omit salt.

Twisted Shapings

Using half of the dough, roll into 12-inch square. Spread with 1 tablespoon butter or margarine, softened. Fold square in half. Cut into 24 strips, each about ½ inch wide and 6 inches long. Shape strips on greased baking sheet as directed below.

2 dozen rolls.

Figure 8's Hold one end of strip in each hand and twist in opposite directions, stretching strip slightly. Bring ends together and shape into figure 8.

French Knots Tie a loose knot in one end of strip; pull longer end of strip through center of knot.

Figure 8's

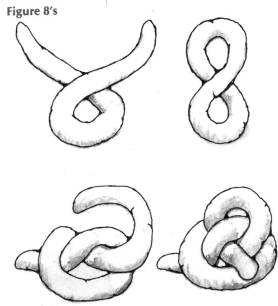

French Knots

Shapings

Cloverleafs   Using half of the dough, shape bits into 1-inch balls, tucking edges under so they resemble mushroom caps. Place 3 balls in each greased muffin cup. Brush rolls with butter. (Pictured on page 39.)

1 dozen rolls.

Fan Tans   Using half of the dough, roll into rectangle, 13x9 inches. Spread with butter. Cut crosswise into 6 strips 1½ inches wide. Stack strips evenly, one on top of the other; cut into 12 pieces about 1 inch wide. Place cut sides down in greased muffin cups. Brush rolls with butter. (Pictured on page 39.)

1 dozen rolls.

Pan Biscuits   Using all of the dough, roll into rectangle, 13x9 inches. Place in greased oblong baking pan, 13x9x2 inches. Score dough ¼ inch deep into 15 rolls. Brush rolls with butter.

15 rolls.

Parker House   Using half of the dough, roll into rectangle, 13x9 inches. Cut into 3-inch circles. Brush with butter. Make crease across each circle; fold so top half overlaps slightly. Press edges together. Place close together in greased 9-inch pie pan. Brush rolls with butter.

10 rolls.

Cloverleafs

Fan Tans

Pan Biscuits

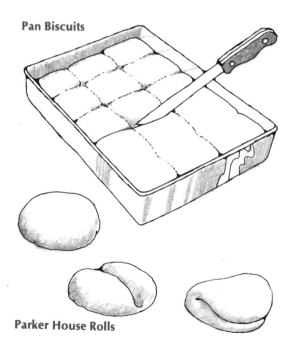

Parker House Rolls

Double-Quick Dinner Rolls

No need to knead or shape. With this dough in the refrigerator, you can start late in the day and still have freshly baked rolls when dinner is served.

1 package active dry yeast
1 cup warm water (105 to 115°)
2 tablespoons sugar
1 teaspoon salt
1 egg
2 tablespoons shortening
2¼ cups all-purpose* or
    unbleached flour

Dissolve yeast in warm water in large mixer bowl. Add sugar, salt, egg, shortening and 1 cup of the flour. Beat until smooth. Stir in remaining flour; continue stirring until smooth. Scrape batter from side of bowl. Cover; let rise in warm place until double, about 30 minutes.

Stir down batter. Spoon into 12 greased large muffin cups, filling each about ½ full. Let rise until batter reaches tops of cups, 20 to 30 minutes.

Heat oven to 400°. Bake 15 minutes.

1 dozen rolls.

*If using self-rising flour, omit salt.

Variation

Hamburger Buns Increase flour to 2¾ cups. After stirring down batter, turn onto floured surface. Divide into 12 equal parts. Shape each part into a smooth ball with lightly greased fingers. Place about 1 inch apart on greased baking sheet. Let rise until double, 20 to 30 minutes. Beat 1 egg yolk and 1 tablespoon water slightly; brush over buns. Sprinkle with finely chopped onion, sesame seed or poppy seed. Bake as directed.

1 dozen buns.

Steps To Good Yeast Rolls

Since they offer such delightful variety, rolls are often considered the "playground of yeast baking." One basic recipe can turn into many different shapes. The steps to good yeast rolls are similar to bread:

Knead the dough about 5 minutes. Allow the dough to rise until doubled (about 1½ hours).

Shape, let rise and bake according to the particular recipe.

The one main difference:

Dough for rolls should be softer than for bread. Add the flour slowly, using *just* enough so the dough can be handled without sticking.

Easy Refrigerator Roll Dough

2 packages active dry yeast
2 cups warm water (105 to 115°)
½ cup sugar
¼ cup shortening
1 egg
2 teaspoons salt
6½ to 7 cups all-purpose* or
    unbleached flour

Dissolve yeast in warm water in large mixer bowl. Stir in sugar, shortening, egg, salt and 3 cups of the flour. Beat until smooth. Stir in enough remaining flour to make dough easy to handle.

Place dough in greased bowl; turn greased side up. Cover loosely with plastic wrap; refrigerate at least 2 hours or until ready to use. (Dough can be kept up to 4 days in refrigerator at 45° or below. Keep covered.)

Punch down dough; divide, shape on lightly floured surface and let rise as directed below. Heat oven to 400°. Bake as directed.

*If using self-rising flour, omit salt.

Shapings

Cheese Crescents Using ¼ of the dough, roll into 12-inch circle. Sprinkle with 3 tablespoons grated Parmesan cheese or American cheese food. Cut into 16 wedges. Roll up each wedge, beginning at rounded edge. Place rolls with points underneath on lightly greased baking sheet; curve to form crescents. Cover; let rise in warm place until double, about 45 minutes. Bake until rolls are golden brown, about 12 minutes.

16 rolls.

Cobblestone Rolls Using ¼ of the dough, shape bits into 1-inch balls, tucking edges under so they resemble mushroom caps. Place in lightly greased 8-inch round layer pan or pie pan. Cover; let rise in warm place until double, about 1 hour. Brush 1 tablespoon butter or margarine, melted, over rolls. Bake until rolls are golden brown, about 15 minutes.

18 rolls.

Cocktail Buns Using all of the dough, shape bits into 1-inch balls, tucking edges under so they resemble mushroom caps. Beat 1 egg yolk and 2 tablespoons water slightly; dip tops of balls into egg mixture, then into poppy seed or sesame seed. Place 1 inch apart on lightly greased baking sheet. Cover; let rise in warm place until double, 1 to 1½ hours. Bake until rolls are golden brown, about 10 minutes.

About 5 dozen buns.

Wheat Germ Biscuits

1 package active dry yeast
1 cup warm water (105 to 115°)
¼ cup brown sugar (packed)
1½ teaspoons salt
½ cup wheat germ
1 egg
3 tablespoons shortening
2¾ to 3¼ cups all-purpose* or
   unbleached flour

Dissolve yeast in warm water in large mixer bowl. Stir in sugar, salt, wheat germ, egg, shortening and 1¾ cups of the flour. Beat until smooth. Stir in enough remaining flour to make dough easy to handle.

Place dough in greased bowl; turn greased side up. Cover; let rise in warm place until double, about 1½ hours. (Dough is ready if an indentation remains when touched.)

Punch down dough. Shape bits of the dough into 1½-inch balls with greased hands (dough is slightly sticky). Place in 2 greased round layer pans, 9x1½ inches. Let rise until double, about 45 minutes.

Heat oven to 375°. Bake until biscuits are brown, 20 to 25 minutes.

2 dozen biscuits.

*If using self-rising flour, omit salt.

Fresh Chive-Yogurt Buns

Simple to make batter buns . . . delightfully different. There's the zippy flavor of yogurt accented with snippets of chives. Just the kind of "How-did-you-do-it?" recipe that sparks dinner table compliments.

1 carton (8 ounces) unflavored
   yogurt (1 cup)
1 package active dry yeast
¼ cup warm water (105 to 115°)
2 tablespoons sugar
1 teaspoon salt
2 tablespoons shortening
1 egg
1 to 2 tablespoons snipped chives
2¼ cups all-purpose* or
   unbleached flour

Heat yogurt *just* to lukewarm. Dissolve yeast in warm water in large mixer bowl. Add yogurt, sugar, salt, shortening, egg, chives and 1½ cups of the flour. Beat until smooth. Stir in remaining flour; continue stirring until smooth. Cover; let rise in warm place until double, about 45 minutes.

Grease 16 medium muffin cups. Stir down batter. Fill muffin cups ½ full. Pat tops of buns to level with floured fingers (batter is sticky-smooth). Let rise until batter reaches tops of cups, 20 to 30 minutes.

Heat oven to 400°. Bake until buns are golden brown, 15 to 20 minutes.

16 buns.

*If using self-rising flour, omit salt.

Harvest Rolls

When the first frost inspires you to bake up something hot and hearty, try these sweet potato–raisin crescents. Perfect for Thanksgiving, too. "May I use *canned* sweets, warmed and mashed?" Yes, if they're vacuum-packed.

   1 package active dry yeast
1½ cups warm water (105 to 115°)
   ⅓ cup sugar
1½ teaspoons salt
   ⅔ cup shortening
   2 eggs
   1 cup lukewarm mashed sweet
      potatoes
   ½ cup raisins
   7 to 7½ cups all-purpose* or
      unbleached flour
      Butter or margarine, softened

Dissolve yeast in warm water in large mixing bowl. Stir in sugar, salt, shortening, eggs, sweet potatoes, raisins and 3 cups of the flour; beat thoroughly. Stir in enough of the remaining flour to make dough easy to handle.

Turn dough onto lightly floured surface; knead until smooth and elastic, about 5 minutes. Place in greased bowl; turn greased side up. Cover; let rise in warm place until double, about 1 hour. (Dough is ready if an indentation remains when touched.) Or cover bowl tightly and refrigerate at least 8 hours. (Dough can be kept up to 3 days in refrigerator at 45° or below. Keep covered.)

Punch down dough; divide into 4 equal parts. Roll each part into a 12-inch circle. Spread with butter. Cut into 16 wedges. Roll up each wedge, beginning at rounded edge. Place rolls with points underneath on greased baking sheet; curve to form crescents. Brush with butter. Let rise until light, about 1 hour.

Heat oven to 400°. Bake until rolls are golden brown, 15 to 20 minutes.

64 rolls.

*If using self-rising flour, omit salt.

What To Do If . . .

You're interrupted in the midst of making bread? If you're called away while beating or kneading the dough, just pick up where you left off. Dough will wait as long as 15 minutes.

You can't shape the dough after it has doubled? Just punch it down to get out the air, cover and let rise again. (The next rising will take a bit less time.)

Shaped dough rises a little too high before you get it in the oven? Turn it out, press out the air bubbles, reshape and let rise again before baking.

Soft Pretzels

1 package active dry yeast
1½ cups warm water (105 to 115°)
1 teaspoon salt
1 teaspoon sugar
3½ to 4 cups all-purpose* or
    unbleached flour
1 egg, beaten
    Coarse salt
    Prepared mustard (optional)

Dissolve yeast in warm water in large mixing bowl. Stir in 1 teaspoon salt, the sugar and 2 cups of the flour. Beat until smooth. Stir in enough remaining flour to make dough easy to handle.

Turn dough onto lightly floured surface; knead until smooth and elastic, about 5 min-utes. Place in greased bowl; turn greased side up. Cover; let rise until double, 45 to 60 minutes. (Dough is ready if an indentation remains when touched.)

Heat oven to 425°. Punch down dough; cut into 16 equal parts. Roll each part into a rope 18 inches long. Twist each rope into a pretzel shape; place on greased baking sheet. Brush pretzels with beaten egg and sprinkle with coarse salt.

Bake until pretzels are brown, 15 to 20 min-utes; cool on wire rack. Eat with mustard. Store pretzels in container with loose-fitting cover. (Pictured on page 39.)

16 pretzels.

*If using self-rising flour, omit 1 teaspoon salt.

Water Bagels

Bagel lovers are sternly partisan: Some prefer their chewy, doughnut-shaped rolls plain; others, livened with the extra richness of egg. We stand neutral and offer both kinds.

1 package active dry yeast
1 cup warm water (105 to 115°)
2 tablespoons sugar
1½ teaspoons salt
2¾ cups all-purpose* or
    unbleached flour
2 quarts water

Dissolve yeast in 1 cup warm water in large mixing bowl. Stir in sugar, salt and 1¼ cups of the flour. Beat until smooth. Stir in remaining flour.

Turn dough onto lightly floured surface; knead until smooth and elastic, about 10 minutes. Place in greased bowl; turn greased side up. Cover; let rise in warm place until double, about 15 minutes. (Dough is ready if an indentation remains when touched.)

Punch down dough; divide into 8 equal parts. Roll each part into a rope 6 inches long; moisten ends with water and pinch to form a bagel. Or shape each part into a smooth ball; punch hole in center and pull gently to enlarge hole and make uniform shape. Let rise 20 minutes. Heat oven to 375°.

Heat 2 quarts water to boiling in large kettle. Reduce heat; add 4 bagels. Simmer 7 minutes, turning once. Drain on kitchen towel. Repeat with remaining bagels, simmering four at a time. Bake on greased baking sheet until bagels are golden brown, 30 to 35 minutes; cool. Serve with cream cheese and lox, or toast and spread with marmalade. (Pictured on page 39.)

8 bagels.

*Do not use self-rising flour in this recipe.

Variation

Egg Bagels With the first addition of flour, add 2 eggs and 2 tablespoons salad oil; increase total amount of flour to 4 cups. Knead 5 minutes. Let rise until double, about 45 minutes. Divide dough into 16 equal parts; shape and let rise as directed. Add 2 tablespoons sugar to boiling water. Simmer 4 minutes, turning once. Beat 1 egg yolk and 1 tablespoon water slightly; brush over simmered bagels. Bake as directed.

16 bagels.

Italian Breadsticks

1 package active dry yeast
⅔ cup warm water (105 to 115°)
1 tablespoon sugar
1 teaspoon salt
¼ cup salad oil or olive oil
2 to 2¼ cups all-purpose* or
   unbleached flour
   Salad oil or olive oil
1 egg white
1 tablespoon water
   Coarse salt or toasted sesame seed

Dissolve yeast in warm water in large mixing bowl. Stir in sugar, 1 teaspoon salt, ¼ cup oil and 1 cup of the flour. Beat until smooth. Stir in enough remaining flour to make dough easy to handle.

Turn dough onto lightly floured surface; knead until smooth and elastic, about 5 minutes. Shape dough into uniform roll 10 inches long. Cut into 32 equal parts. Roll each part into a pencillike rope, 8 inches long for thick breadsticks, or 10 inches long for thin breadsticks. Place 1 inch apart on greased baking sheets. Brush lightly with oil. Cover; let rise in warm place 20 minutes.

Heat oven to 350°. Beat egg white and 1 tablespoon water slightly; brush over sticks and sprinkle with coarse salt. Bake until breadsticks are golden brown, 20 to 25 minutes. (Pictured on page 39.)

32 breadsticks.

*If using self-rising flour, omit 1 teaspoon salt.

English Muffins

1 package active dry yeast
1 cup warm water (105 to 115°)
2 teaspoons salt
1 teaspoon sugar
¼ cup shortening
3 cups all-purpose* or
   unbleached flour
2 tablespoons cornmeal

Dissolve yeast in warm water in large mixing bowl. Add salt, sugar, shortening and flour. Stir until smooth. Roll dough ¼ inch thick on floured surface. Cut into 3½-inch circles.

Sprinkle ungreased baking sheet with 1 tablespoon cornmeal; place circles on baking sheet. Sprinkle remaining 1 tablespoon cornmeal over circles. Cover; let rise in warm place until light, about 1 hour. (Dough is ready if an indentation remains when touched.)

Heat ungreased electric griddle or skillet to 375°. Transfer circles to griddle. Cook 7 minutes on each side; cool. To serve, split, toast and spread with butter and marmalade. (Pictured on page 39.)

10 to 12 muffins.

*If using self-rising flour, omit salt.

Pictured on page 39: Clockwise from upper left – Fan Tans (page 31), Italian Breadsticks (page 38), Water Bagels (page 37), Cloverleafs (page 31), English Muffins (page 38), Soft Pretzels (page 36).
Pictured on page 40: Croissants (page 41).

Croissants

As a welcome antidote to the hurry-scurry of today's world, this rich French-inspired crescent roll stands supreme. Butter, lavished between thin layers of dough, produces a delicate flakiness and meltingly good flavor.

  2 packages active dry yeast
½ cup warm water (105 to 115°)
⅔ cup lukewarm milk (scalded, then
     cooled)
¼ cup salad oil
  3 tablespoons sugar
  2 teaspoons salt
  2 eggs
3½ to 4 cups all-purpose* or
     unbleached flour
  1 cup butter, softened**
  1 egg white
  1 tablespoon water

Dissolve yeast in warm water in large mixing bowl. Stir in milk, oil, sugar, salt, eggs and 2 cups of the flour. Beat until smooth. Stir in enough remaining flour to make dough easy to handle.

Turn dough onto lightly floured surface; knead until smooth and elastic, about 5 minutes. Place in greased bowl; turn greased side up. Cover; let rise in warm place until double. (Dough is ready if an indentation remains when touched.)

Punch down dough. Cover; refrigerate 1 hour.

Punch down dough. Roll into rectangle, 25x10 inches. Spread with ⅓ cup of the butter. Fold crosswise into thirds, overlapping the 2 sides to make 3 layers; roll out. Repeat 2 times, spreading rectangle with ⅓ cup butter each time. Divide dough in half; refrigerate 1 hour.

Shape half of the dough at a time (keep other half refrigerated). Roll into rectangle, 12x8 inches. Cut lengthwise in half; then cut crosswise into 3 squares. Cut each square diagonally into 2 triangles.

Roll up each triangle, beginning at long side. Place rolls with points underneath on ungreased baking sheet; curve to form crescents. Refrigerate 30 minutes.

Heat oven to 425°. Beat egg white and 1 tablespoon water slightly; brush over croissants. Bake until croissants are brown and crisp, 14 to 16 minutes. (Pictured on page 40.)

2 dozen croissants.

 *Do not use self-rising flour in this recipe.
**Do not use margarine in this recipe.

Buckwheat Flapjacks

1 package active dry yeast
¼ cup warm water (105 to 115°)
1¾ cups lukewarm milk (scalded, then cooled)
2 tablespoons brown sugar
1 teaspoon salt
3 eggs
¼ cup butter or margarine, softened
1 cup buckwheat flour
1 cup all-purpose* or unbleached flour

Dissolve yeast in warm water in large mixing bowl. Add remaining ingredients; beat until smooth. Cover; let rise in warm place 1½ hours. Stir down batter. Cover; refrigerate at least 8 hours. (Batter can be kept up to 12 hours in refrigerator.)

Stir down batter. Grease heated griddle if necessary. Pour batter from ¼-cup measuring cup or from tip of large spoon onto hot griddle. Turn flapjacks as soon as they are puffed and full of bubbles, but turn before bubbles break. Cook until flapjacks are golden brown on other side.

About sixteen 4-inch flapjacks.

*If using self-rising flour, omit salt.

Variations

Buckwheat Waffles Pour batter from cup or pitcher onto center of hot waffle iron. Cook until steaming stops, about 5 minutes. Remove waffle carefully.

About eight 7-inch waffles.

Whole Wheat Flapjacks and Waffles Substitute stone-ground whole wheat flour for the buckwheat flour.

The Sweet Side

Here are the kinds of special recipes that are nice to share. For special occasions or holidays or simply to say that this is no ordinary day. Take your pick of tempting sweet rolls, coffee cakes and festive breads. All sweet ways to say, "Come on over for coffee and...."

Traditional Sweet Dough

Roll it, slice it, "ring" it! Variations on the basic sweet dough theme are so delicious, be prepared to double the recipe, refrigerate the dough and rejoice in baking up fresh surprises for 3 or 4 days running.

  1 package active dry yeast
¼ cup warm water (105 to 115°)
¼ cup lukewarm milk (scalded, then cooled)
¼ cup sugar
½ teaspoon salt
  1 egg
¼ cup shortening
2¼ to 2½ cups all-purpose* or unbleached flour

Dissolve yeast in warm water in large mixing bowl. Stir in milk, sugar, salt, egg, shortening and 1¼ cups of the flour. Beat until smooth. Stir in enough remaining flour to make dough easy to handle.

Turn dough onto lightly floured surface; knead until smooth and elastic, about 5 minutes. Place in greased bowl; turn greased side up. (At this point, dough can be kept 3 to 4 days in refrigerator at 45° or below. Keep covered.) Cover; let rise in warm place until double, about 1½ hours. (Dough is ready if an indentation remains when touched.)

Punch down dough; shape, let rise and bake as directed in the following recipes.

*If using self-rising flour, omit salt.

Note: This recipe can be doubled.

Butterscotch Pecan Rolls

½ cup butter or margarine
½ cup brown sugar (packed)
½ cup pecan halves
    Traditional Sweet Dough (left)
  2 tablespoons butter or margarine, softened
¼ cup granulated sugar
  2 teaspoons cinnamon

Melt ½ cup butter in oblong baking pan, 13x9x2 inches. Stir in brown sugar and pecan halves.

Roll dough into rectangle, 15x9 inches, on lightly floured surface. Spread with 2 tablespoons butter; sprinkle with granulated sugar and cinnamon. Roll up tightly, beginning at one of the long sides. Pinch edge of dough into roll to seal. Stretch and shape until even.

Cut roll into 15 slices about 1 inch wide. Place slices slightly apart in pan. Let rise until double, about 45 minutes.

Heat oven to 375°. Bake until rolls are brown, 25 to 30 minutes. Immediately invert pan on large tray. Let pan remain over rolls a minute so butter-sugar mixture will drizzle down.

15 rolls.

Sugar Crisps

Traditional Sweet Dough (facing page)
Butter or margarine, melted
1 cup sugar
1 cup finely chopped pecans

Roll dough into rectangle, 18x9 inches, on lightly floured surface. Brush with butter. Mix sugar and pecans; sprinkle half of the mixture over rectangle.

Roll up, beginning at one of the long sides. Pinch edge of dough into roll to seal. Cut roll into 18 slices about 1 inch wide. Sprinkle remaining sugar-nut mixture onto board and roll and flatten each slice into a 4-inch circle.

Place rolls on greased baking sheets. Let rise until double, about 30 minutes. Heat oven to 375°. Bake until rolls are done, about 10 minutes.

18 rolls.

Which Yeast To Use—Dry or Cake?

Although they can be used interchangeably, active dry yeast stays fresh for months on the shelf. (Look for the expiration date on the back of the packet.) Compressed yeast must be refrigerated and used within a week or so. When in doubt, crumble some of the cake in your fingers. If it crumbles easily, it's still good.

Swedish Tea Ring

Traditional Sweet Dough (facing page)
2 tablespoons butter or margarine, softened
½ cup brown sugar (packed)
2 teaspoons cinnamon
½ cup raisins
Confectioners' Sugar Icing (below)

Roll dough into rectangle, 15x9 inches, on lightly floured surface. Spread with butter. Mix sugar, cinnamon and raisins; sprinkle over dough. Roll up tightly, beginning at one of the long sides. Pinch edge of dough into roll to seal. Stretch and shape until even.

Place roll seam side down on lightly greased baking sheet. Shape into ring; pinch ends together. With scissors, make cuts ⅔ of the way through ring at 1-inch intervals. Turn each section on its side. Let rise until double, about 45 minutes.

Heat oven to 375°. Bake until coffee cake is done, 25 to 30 minutes. While warm, frost with Confectioners' Sugar Icing and, if desired, decorate with nuts and cherries.

1 coffee cake.

Confectioners' Sugar Icing
Mix 1 cup confectioners' sugar and about 1 tablespoon milk until smooth.

Brown Sugar Sweet Dough

Brown sugar and crunchy oats, adaptable starters for a trio of superb bakings: Rolls whirled with granola and cinnamon; coffee cake pocketed with apples and raisins; crescents jeweled with fruit, nuts and preserves.

 2 packages active dry yeast
½ cup warm water (105 to 115°)
½ cup lukewarm milk (scalded, then cooled)
½ cup brown sugar (packed)
 1 teaspoon salt
 2 eggs
½ cup butter or margarine, softened
 1 cup uncooked quick rolled oats
3½ to 4 cups all-purpose* or unbleached flour

Dissolve yeast in warm water in large mixing bowl. Stir in milk, sugar, salt, eggs, butter, oats and 1½ cups of the flour. Beat until smooth. Stir in enough remaining flour to make dough easy to handle.

Turn dough onto lightly floured surface; knead until smooth and elastic, about 5 minutes. Place in greased bowl; turn greased side up. Cover; let rise in warm place until double, about 1½ hours. (Dough is ready if an indentation remains when touched.)

Punch down dough; divide in half. Shape, let rise and bake as directed in the following recipes.

*If using self-rising flour, omit salt.

Granola-Cinnamon Rolls

½ Brown Sugar Sweet Dough (left)
 2 tablespoons butter or margarine, softened
½ cup granola without fruit*
¼ cup brown sugar (packed)
 2 teaspoons cinnamon
    Quick White Icing (facing page)

Roll dough into rectangle, 15x9 inches, on lightly floured surface. Spread with butter. Mix granola, sugar and cinnamon; sprinkle over rectangle. Roll up, beginning at one of the long sides. Pinch edge of dough into roll to seal. Stretch and shape until even.

Cut roll into 15 slices about 1 inch wide. Place slices slightly apart in greased square baking pan, 9x9x2 inches, or in greased muffin cups. Let rise until double, about 45 minutes.

Heat oven to 350°. Bake until rolls are brown, 25 to 30 minutes. While warm, frost with Quick White Icing.

15 rolls.

*A mixture of ¼ cup uncooked quick rolled oats and ¼ cup flaked coconut can be substituted for the granola.

Apple-Raisin Coffee Cake

   2 medium red apples
  ½ cup raisins
  ½ cup granulated sugar
  ⅓ cup light corn syrup
  ½ teaspoon cinnamon
  ½ Brown Sugar Sweet Dough
     (facing page)
     Milk
     Crumbled Topping (below)
     Quick White Icing (right)

Core and finely chop apples. Combine apples, raisins, sugar, corn syrup and cinnamon in saucepan. Cook, stirring frequently, until mixture is consistency of thick jam, about 10 minutes. Cool thoroughly.

Cut dough into 12 equal parts. Press each part into a 4-inch square on floured surface. Place 1 level tablespoon filling in center. Bring 2 opposite corners together. Moisten with milk; overlap about 1 inch and pinch to seal. Repeat with remaining 2 corners.

Place filled squares slightly apart in greased square baking pan, 9x9x2 inches. Sprinkle with Crumbled Topping. Let rise until double, about 45 minutes.

Heat oven to 350°. Bake until coffee cake is golden brown, 25 to 30 minutes. While warm, frost with Quick White Icing.

1 coffee cake.

Crumbled Topping
Mix 2 tablespoons each firm butter or margarine, brown sugar, uncooked quick rolled oats and flour and ¼ teaspoon vanilla with fork until crumbly.

Quick White Icing
Mix 1 cup confectioners' sugar, 1 tablespoon water or milk and ½ teaspoon vanilla until smooth.

Strawberry-Apricot Crescents

  ½ cup strawberry preserves
  ½ cup finely cut-up dried apricots
  ¼ cup finely chopped nuts
  ½ Brown Sugar Sweet Dough
     (facing page)
     Quick White Icing (above)

Mix strawberry preserves, apricots and nuts. Roll dough into 12-inch circle on lightly floured surface. Spread with strawberry mixture. Cut into 16 wedges. Roll up each wedge, beginning at rounded edge.

Place rolls with points underneath on greased baking sheet; curve to form crescents. Let rise until double, about 45 minutes.

Heat oven to 350°. Bake until rolls are golden brown, 20 to 25 minutes. While warm, frost with Quick White Icing.

16 rolls.

Orange Sweet Dough

Consider this memory-making orange dough as a golden treasure and spend it as you please. Will you have gingery coffee cake? Cinnamon swirls? Citrus-flavored pinwheels? All with the rich taste of sunshine.

  2 packages active dry yeast
  1 cup warm water (105 to 115°)
  1 tablespoon grated orange peel
  1 cup orange juice
  ½ cup sugar
  2 teaspoons salt
  1 egg
  ¼ cup butter or margarine, softened
  6½ to 7 cups all-purpose* or unbleached flour

Dissolve yeast in warm water in large mixer bowl. Add orange peel, orange juice, sugar, salt, egg, butter and 3 cups of the flour. Beat ½ minute on low speed, scraping bowl constantly. Beat 2 minutes on medium speed, scraping bowl occasionally. Stir in enough remaining flour to make dough easy to handle.

Cover; let rise in warm place until double, about 1½ hours. (Dough is ready if an indentation remains when touched.)

Punch down dough; divide in half. Shape, let rise and bake as directed in the following recipes.

*If using self-rising flour, omit salt.

Orange-Almond Ripple Loaf

  ½ cup sugar
  ½ cup sliced almonds
  1 tablespoon grated orange peel
  1 tablespoon chopped crystallized ginger
  ½ Orange Sweet Dough (left)
  2 tablespoons butter or margarine, softened
    Streusel Topping (below)

Mix sugar, almonds, orange peel and ginger. Roll dough into rectangle, 16x10 inches, on lightly floured surface. Spread with butter; sprinkle with sugar-almond mixture.

Cut crosswise into 4 strips about 4 inches wide. Stack strips evenly, one on top of the other; cut into 5 pieces about 2 inches wide.

Place strips cut sides down in row in greased loaf pan, 9x5x3 or 8½x4½x2½ inches. Sprinkle with Streusel Topping. Let rise until double, about 45 minutes. Heat oven to 375°. Bake until coffee cake is golden brown, 25 to 30 minutes.

1 coffee cake.

Streusel Topping
Mix 2 tablespoons flour, 2 tablespoons sugar and 1 tablespoon firm butter or margarine with fork until crumbly.

Orange-Cinnamon Rolls

¼ cup sugar
2 teaspoons cinnamon
½ Orange Sweet Dough (facing page)
2 tablespoons butter or margarine, softened

Mix sugar and cinnamon. Roll dough into rectangle, 15x9 inches, on lightly floured surface. Spread with butter; sprinkle with sugar and cinnamon. Roll up, beginning at one of the long sides. Pinch edge of dough into roll to seal well. Stretch roll to make even.

Cut roll into 15 slices about 1 inch wide. Place slices slightly apart in greased oblong baking pan, 13x9x2 inches, or in greased muffin cups. Let rise until double, about 30 minutes.

Heat oven to 375°. Bake until rolls are golden brown, 25 to 30 minutes. If desired, while warm frost with mixture of 1 cup confectioners' sugar, 1 tablespoon orange juice and ½ teaspoon vanilla.

15 rolls.

Bake Ahead . . . and Freeze!

When a coffee cake or some sweet rolls are waiting in the freezer, company can drop in *any* time. So be glad for a recipe that bakes up more than one. For how-to tips on freezing and thawing, see page 71.

Orange Pinwheels

3 tablespoons butter or margarine, softened
1 tablespoon grated orange peel
2 tablespoons orange juice
1½ cups confectioners' sugar
½ Orange Sweet Dough (facing page)

Beat butter, orange peel, orange juice and confectioners' sugar until creamy and smooth. Roll dough into rectangle, 15x9 inches, on lightly floured surface.

Spread with half of the orange filling. Roll up, beginning at one of the long sides. Pinch edge of dough into roll to seal. Stretch and shape until even.

Cut roll into 15 slices about 1 inch wide. Place slices slightly apart in greased oblong baking pan, 13x9x2 inches, or in greased muffin cups. Let rise until double, about 30 minutes.

Heat oven to 375°. Bake 25 minutes. While warm, frost with remaining filling. (Pictured on page 65.)

15 rolls.

Home-Style Refrigerator Dough

Almost every country has its special baking made with satiny, long-keeping mashed-potato dough. In Yugoslavia it's Poteca; in Germany, Cheese Kuchen. Why not start with Easter Egg Rolls and go on from there.

1 package active dry yeast
1½ cups warm water (105 to 115°)
⅔ cup sugar
1½ teaspoons salt
⅔ cup shortening
2 eggs
1 cup lukewarm mashed potatoes*
7 to 7½ cups all-purpose** or unbleached flour

Dissolve yeast in warm water in large mixing bowl. Stir in sugar, salt, shortening, eggs, potatoes and 4 cups of the flour. Beat until smooth. Stir in enough remaining flour to make dough easy to handle.

Turn dough onto lightly floured surface; knead until smooth and elastic, about 5 minutes. Place in greased bowl; turn greased side up. Cover tightly; refrigerate at least 8 hours. (Dough can be kept up to 5 days in refrigerator at 45° or below. Keep covered.)

Punch down dough; divide, shape, let rise and bake as directed in the following recipes.

*Instant mashed potato puffs can be used; prepare as directed for 2 servings.
**If using self-rising flour, omit salt.

Easter Egg Rolls

¼ Home-Style Refrigerator Dough (left)
Butter or margarine, softened
1 cup confectioners' sugar
1 tablespoon water or milk
½ teaspoon vanilla
2 to 3 drops food color
Candies

Shape bits of the dough into 1-inch balls, tucking edges under so they resemble mushroom caps. Place in lightly greased round layer pan, 9x1½ inches. Brush with butter.

Cover dough; let rise in warm place until double, about 1½ hours. (Dough is ready if an indentation remains when touched.)

Heat oven to 400°. Bake until rolls are light brown, about 20 minutes; cool on wire rack (do not separate).

Mix sugar, water and vanilla until smooth. Stir in food color to make a tinted icing. Use in Easy Paper Decorators' Tube (below) to decorate each roll as an Easter egg and use candies to make names, borders, flowers and leaves.

3 dozen rolls.

Easy Paper Decorators' Tube: Cut off tiny corner of an envelope. Fill with about ⅓ cup icing at a time. Use as a pastry tube.

Kaese Kuchen (Cheese Kuchen)

½ Home-Style Refrigerator Dough (facing page)
1½ cups dry cottage cheese
3 eggs
1 teaspoon vanilla
2 tablespoons flour
1 cup cut-up dates
½ cup chopped nuts
½ cup sugar
¼ cup sugar
1 teaspoon cinnamon

Pat dough in greased oblong baking pan, 13x9x2 inches, building up ridge around edges. Cover; let rise in warm place until double, about 1½ hours. (Dough is ready if an indentation remains when touched.)

Heat oven to 375°. Mix cottage cheese, eggs, vanilla, flour, dates, nuts and ½ cup sugar. Spread over dough up to ridge. Mix ¼ cup sugar and the cinnamon; sprinkle over filling.

Bake 15 minutes. Decrease oven temperature to 325°. Bake until crust is golden brown, 30 to 35 minutes.

1 coffee cake.

Poteca

¼ Home-Style Refrigerator Dough (facing page)
1 cup very finely chopped walnuts
¼ cup brown sugar (packed)
2 tablespoons butter or margarine, softened
1 egg
¼ teaspoon vanilla
¼ teaspoon lemon extract
Butter or margarine, softened

Roll dough into rectangle, 15x10 inches, on lightly floured surface. Mix walnuts, sugar, 2 tablespoons butter, the egg, vanilla and lemon extract. Spread over rectangle to within 1 inch of edges.

Roll up gently, beginning at one of the long sides. Moisten ends with water; pinch edge of dough into roll to seal. Stretch and shape until even. Coil around to form a snail shape.

Place coffee cake seam side down in greased square baking pan, 9x9x2 inches. Cover; let rise in warm place until double, about 1½ hours. (Dough is ready if an indentation remains when touched.)

Heat oven to 375°. Bake until coffee cake is brown, 30 to 35 minutes. While warm, brush with butter.

1 coffee cake.

Kolaches

2 packages active dry yeast
½ cup warm water (105 to 115°)
½ cup lukewarm milk (scalded, then cooled)
½ cup sugar
1 teaspoon salt
4 egg yolks or 2 eggs
⅔ cup butter or margarine, softened
4½ to 5 cups all-purpose* or unbleached flour
Prune-Apricot Filling or Poppy Seed Filling (right)

Dissolve yeast in warm water in large mixing bowl. Stir in milk, sugar, salt, egg yolks, butter and 2 cups of the flour. Beat until smooth. Stir in enough remaining flour to make dough easy to handle.

Turn dough onto lightly floured surface; knead until smooth and elastic, about 5 minutes. Place in greased bowl; turn greased side up. Cover; let rise in warm place until double, about 1½ hours. (Dough is ready if an indentation remains when touched.)

Punch down dough; divide into 24 equal parts. Shape each part into a smooth ball, tucking edge under so it resembles a mushroom cap. Place 12 balls about 2 inches apart on each of 2 greased baking sheets.

Make depression in center of each ball with fingers by pushing outward toward edge, leaving ½-inch ridge around outside of circle. Fill with about 1 tablespoon filling. Let rise until double, about 30 minutes.

Heat oven to 350°. Bake until kolaches are light brown, 15 to 18 minutes.

2 dozen kolaches.

*If using self-rising flour, omit salt.

Prune-Apricot Filling

1 cup pitted prunes
¾ cup dried apricots
1 tablespoon grated lemon peel
1 tablespoon lemon juice
½ cup sugar
¼ teaspoon allspice

Simmer prunes and apricots in enough water to cover until tender, about 30 minutes. Drain; finely chop fruit. Mix in remaining ingredients; cool.

Poppy Seed Filling

½ cup crushed poppy seed
⅓ cup dairy sour cream
¼ cup chopped almonds
¼ cup honey
2 tablespoons red currant jelly
1 tablespoon cornstarch
1 tablespoon butter or margarine
1 teaspoon grated lemon peel

Heat all ingredients to boiling, stirring constantly. Boil and stir 1 minute; cool.

Honey-Wheat Twist

Naturally good! A two-toned twist flavored with apple juice, wheat germ and whole wheat flour and coated with honey and almonds. It's a truly modern coffee bread with a good old-fashioned turn.

¾ cup apple juice
⅓ cup wheat germ
2 packages active dry yeast
¼ cup warm water (105 to 115°)
3 tablespoons butter or margarine, softened
¼ cup honey
2 teaspoons salt
1 egg
2¾ to 3 cups all-purpose* or unbleached flour
¾ to 1 cup whole wheat flour
Honey-Almond Glaze (right)

Heat apple juice just to boiling in small saucepan. Stir in wheat germ; cool. Dissolve yeast in warm water in large mixing bowl. Stir in butter, honey, salt, egg, wheat germ–apple juice mixture and 2 cups of the all-purpose flour. Beat until smooth.

Divide dough in half. Stir in enough of the whole wheat flour to one half to form a soft dough. Stir in enough of the remaining all-purpose flour to the other half to form a soft dough.

Turn each half onto lightly floured surface; knead until smooth and elastic, about 5 minutes. Place in greased bowls; turn greased sides up. Cover; let rise in warm place until double, about 1½ hours. (Dough is ready if an indentation remains when touched.)

Punch down dough; roll each half into a rope about 15 inches long. Place ropes side by side on greased baking sheet; twist together gently and loosely. Pinch ends to fasten. Let rise until double, about 1 hour.

Heat oven to 350°. Bake until twist is done, 30 to 35 minutes. Cool slightly; spread with Honey-Almond Glaze. (Pictured on page 65.)

1 twist.

*If using self-rising flour, omit salt.

Honey-Almond Glaze

¼ cup chopped almonds
1 tablespoon butter or margarine
2 tablespoons sugar
¼ cup honey

Cook and stir almonds in butter until almonds are brown. Add sugar and honey; heat to boiling, stirring constantly. Remove from heat; cool.

Twin Coffee Cakes Dough

Identical twins? No, but each of these opulent, fruit-ladened horseshoes is born of the same rich heritage. Bake both from a single batch of sumptuous sour cream dough. Serve one now; keep the other in the freezer, to pop out for "coffee and. . . ."

    1 cup dairy sour cream
    1 package active dry yeast
    ¼ cup warm water (105 to 115°)
    2 tablespoons butter or margarine, softened
    3 tablespoons sugar
    1 teaspoon salt
    1 egg
      About 3 cups all-purpose* or unbleached flour

Heat sour cream just to lukewarm. Dissolve yeast in warm water in large mixing bowl. Stir in sour cream, butter, sugar, salt, egg and 1 cup of the flour. Beat until smooth. Stir in enough remaining flour to make dough easy to handle.

Turn dough onto lightly floured surface; knead until smooth, about 10 minutes. Place in greased bowl; turn greased side up. Cover; let rise in warm place until double, about 1 hour. (Dough is ready if an indentation remains when touched.)

Punch down dough; divide in half. Use half of the dough for each of the following coffee cakes.

*If using self-rising flour, omit salt.

Blueberry-Lemon Coffee Cake

    1 cup fresh or frozen blueberries
    3 tablespoons sugar
    1 tablespoon cornstarch
    1 tablespoon lemon juice
    ½ Twin Coffee Cakes Dough (left)
      Lemon Icing (below)

Combine blueberries, sugar, cornstarch and lemon juice in small saucepan. Cook over medium heat until thickened; cool.

Roll dough into rectangle, 18x6 inches, on lightly floured surface. Spread blueberry mixture over rectangle to within ½ inch of edges. Roll up, beginning at one of the long sides. Pinch edge of dough into roll to seal well. Stretch and shape until even.

Place roll seam side down on lightly greased baking sheet; curve to form horseshoe shape.

Heat oven to 375°. Bake until coffee cake is golden brown, about 20 minutes. While warm, frost with Lemon Icing.

1 coffee cake.

Lemon Icing

Mix ½ cup confectioners' sugar, 1 tablespoon grated lemon peel and 2 teaspoons lemon juice until smooth.

Pineapple Coffee Cake

1 can (13¼ ounces) crushed pineapple, drained (reserve 1 tablespoon plus 1 teaspoon syrup)
2 tablespoons cornstarch
¼ cup brown sugar (packed)
¼ cup sliced almonds
2 tablespoons firm butter or margarine
2 tablespoons brown sugar
¼ cup all-purpose or unbleached flour
¼ cup sliced almonds
½ Twin Coffee Cakes Dough (facing page)
Glaze (right)

Combine pineapple, cornstarch and ¼ cup sugar in small saucepan. Cook over medium heat until thickened; remove from heat. Stir in ¼ cup almonds; cool.

Mix butter, 2 tablespoons sugar and the flour until crumbly. Stir in ¼ cup almonds and set aside.

Roll dough into rectangle, 18x6 inches, on lightly floured surface. Spread pineapple mixture over rectangle to within ½ inch of edges. Roll up, beginning at one of the long sides. Pinch edge of dough into roll to seal well. Stretch and shape until even.

Place roll seam side down on lightly greased baking sheet; curve to form horseshoe shape. With scissors, make a lengthwise cut through top layers of dough. Fold back layers to completely expose filling and double width of coffee cake. Sprinkle with crumbly mixture.

Heat oven to 375°. Bake until coffee cake is golden brown, about 20 minutes. While warm, drizzle with Glaze.

1 coffee cake.

Glaze

Mix ½ cup brown sugar (packed) and the reserved 1 tablespoon plus 1 teaspoon pineapple syrup until smooth.

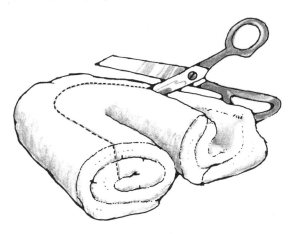

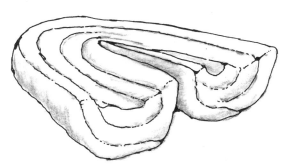

Doughnuts

2 packages active dry yeast
¼ cup warm water (105 to 115°)
1½ cups lukewarm milk (scalded, then cooled)
½ cup sugar
1 teaspoon salt
1 teaspoon nutmeg
¼ teaspoon cinnamon (optional)
2 eggs
⅓ cup shortening
5 cups all-purpose* or unbleached flour
    Granulated sugar, Creamy Glaze or Chocolate Glaze (right)

Dissolve yeast in warm water in large mixer bowl. Add milk, ½ cup sugar, the salt, nutmeg, cinnamon, eggs, shortening and 2 cups of the flour. Blend ½ minute on low speed, scraping bowl constantly. Beat 2 minutes on medium speed, scraping bowl occasionally. Stir in remaining flour; continue stirring until smooth, scraping side of bowl.

Cover; let rise in warm place until double, 50 to 60 minutes. (Dough is ready if an indentation remains when touched.)

Turn dough onto well-floured cloth-covered board; roll around lightly to coat with flour. Gently roll dough ½ inch thick with floured stockinet-covered rolling pin. Cut into 2½-inch doughnuts with floured doughnut cutter (or make a cutter by removing ends from a can about 2½ inches in diameter and using a 1-inch cutter for centers). Cover; let rise on board until double, about 20 minutes.

Heat fat or oil (3 to 4 inches) to 350° in deep fat fryer or kettle. Drop doughnuts into hot fat. Fry until doughnuts are golden brown, 1 to 1½ minutes on each side. Carefully remove from fat; do not prick surface. Drain. While warm, roll doughnuts in sugar or spread with Creamy or Chocolate Glaze.

1 to 1½ dozen doughnuts.

*If using self-rising flour, omit salt.

Creamy Glaze

⅓ cup butter or margarine
2 cups confectioners' sugar
1½ teaspoons vanilla
4 to 6 tablespoons hot water

Melt butter in saucepan; blend in sugar and vanilla. Stir in water, 1 tablespoon at a time, until glaze is spreading consistency.

Enough glaze for about 1 dozen doughnuts.

Chocolate Glaze

4 ounces semisweet chocolate
⅓ cup butter or margarine
2 cups confectioners' sugar
1½ teaspoons vanilla
4 to 6 tablespoons hot water

Melt chocolate and butter over low heat. Remove from heat; blend in sugar and vanilla. Stir in hot water, 1 tablespoon at a time, until glaze is spreading consistency.

Enough glaze for about 1 dozen doughnuts.

Butter Pecan–Apple Coffee Cake

Topping (right)
1 package active dry yeast
¾ cup warm water (105 to 115°)
¼ cup sugar
1 teaspoon salt
1 egg
¼ cup shortening
2¼ cups all-purpose* or
    unbleached flour

Prepare Topping. Dissolve yeast in warm water in large mixer bowl. Add sugar, salt, egg, shortening and 1¼ cups of the flour. Beat 2 minutes on medium speed, scraping bowl frequently. Stir in remaining flour; continue stirring until smooth.

Drop batter by tablespoonfuls onto Topping in pan. Cover; let rise in warm place until double, about 1 hour.

Heat oven to 375°. Bake until coffee cake is golden brown, 30 to 35 minutes. Immediately invert pan on serving plate. Let pan remain on coffee cake a minute so topping will drizzle down.

1 coffee cake.

*If using self-rising flour, omit salt.

Topping
⅓ cup butter or margarine
½ cup whole pecans
½ cup brown sugar (packed)
2 tablespoons light corn syrup
1 teaspoon cinnamon
1 apple, pared, cored and thinly
    sliced

Melt butter in square baking pan, 9x9x2 inches; stir in pecans. Heat until butter is brown and pecans are toasted. Remove from heat and cool. Stir in sugar, corn syrup and cinnamon; spread evenly in pan. Arrange apple slices over butter-nut mixture.

Danish Pastry Dough

¾ cup cold firm butter (1½ sticks)*
2 packages active dry yeast
½ cup warm water (105 to 115°)
¼ cup lukewarm milk (scalded, then cooled)
¼ cup sugar
1 teaspoon salt
2 eggs
3 cups all-purpose** or unbleached flour

Cut whole stick of butter crosswise in half. Place 3 half-sticks butter side by side on piece of waxed paper. Place second piece of waxed paper on top of butter. Flatten butter into 7-inch square with rolling pin so that butter forms a solid sheet. Refrigerate 1½ hours or until dough is ready to be rolled. (Butter must be very cold to prevent sticking when dough is rolled.)

Dissolve yeast in warm water in large mixing bowl. Stir in milk, sugar, salt, eggs and 2 cups of the flour. Beat until smooth. Stir in remaining flour until absorbed. Place dough in lightly greased bowl; cover with damp cloth. Refrigerate 1½ hours (see note).

Place chilled dough on generously floured cloth-covered board. With generously floured stockinet-covered rolling pin, roll dough into 15-inch circle. Place sheet of cold butter in center of dough. Fold right and left edges of dough to center, covering butter. Fold bottom and top edges of dough to center; press down to seal securely. (Dough forms a square envelope around butter.)

Working firmly but gently, roll dough into rectangle, 20x10 inches; dough should be no more than ¼ inch thick. (Dough is stiff at first.) Fold rectangle into thirds, bringing one of the 10-inch ends up ⅔ of the way and folding top third down over bottom third to make 3 layers. Use a pastry brush to remove excess flour from dough while folding. Press down firmly at top and bottom of rectangle to secure dough and seal seam.

Work as quickly as possible so that butter does not soften. Continue flouring cloth generously as needed to prevent dough from sticking. If butter breaks through dough onto cloth, simply flour this area heavily and continue rolling.

Turn rectangle one turn to the left so that bottom right-hand corner becomes upper right-hand corner. Roll dough into rectangle, 20x10 inches. Fold rectangle into thirds. Be careful to keep sides and ends straight—uneven rolling produces less flakiness.

Turn rectangle one turn to the left; repeat rolling process a third time. Fold rectangle a final time; place folded rectangle on flat tray. Cover with plastic wrap; refrigerate until dough is well chilled, 1½ to 2 hours. Divide rectangle in half, cutting perpendicular to fold. Use half of the dough for any of the variations on facing page. Keep remaining half refrigerated until ready to use.

*Do not use margarine in this recipe.
**If using self-rising flour, omit salt.

Twists

Using half of the chilled dough, roll into rectangle, 12x7 inches. Cut into twelve 1-inch strips. Shape into Figure 8's or Snails.

Figure 8's Hold one end of strip in each hand and twist in opposite directions, stretching strip slightly. Bring ends together and shape on ungreased baking sheet into figure 8.

Snails Hold one end of strip on ungreased baking sheet with thumb and wind strip around it. Tuck free end under roll.

Cover rolls; let rise in warm place until double, about 45 minutes. (Dough is ready if an indentation remains when touched.)

Heat oven to 400°. Make a depression in center of each loop of figure 8's or in center of each snail. Fill with 1 teaspoon jam, jelly, preserves or Prune-Apricot Filling (page 52). Bake until rolls are golden brown, 10 to 12 minutes.

1 dozen rolls.

Note: Dough can be refrigerated 8 hours before rolling with butter; cover with plastic wrap to prevent drying out. Punch down and continue as directed.

To freeze, wrap baked pastries in aluminum foil and freeze. To thaw, heat oven to 400°. Open foil package slightly; heat 15 minutes. (A tightly sealed package causes pastry to lose crispness. A completely open package tends to dry pastry.)

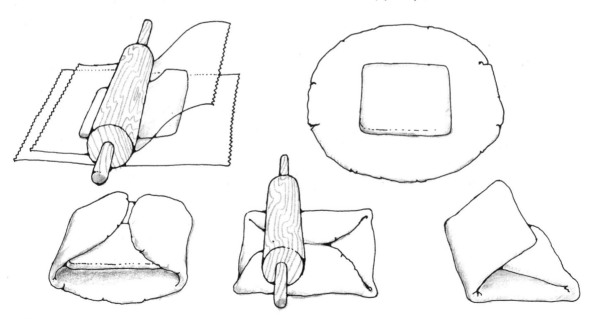

Fans

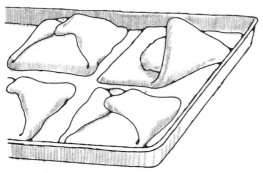

Cream Buns

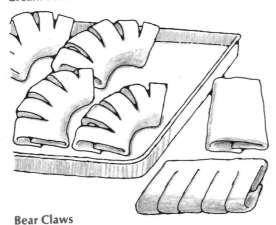

Bear Claws

Fans

½ Danish Pastry Dough (page 58),
 chilled
1 egg white
1 teaspoon water
⅓ cup chopped walnuts
2 tablespoons raisins
2 tablespoons sugar
½ teaspoon cinnamon

Roll dough into rectangle, 16x9 inches, on lightly floured surface. Beat egg white and water slightly; brush over rectangle. Sprinkle with walnuts, raisins and a mixture of sugar and cinnamon. Place piece of waxed paper over rectangle; gently press filling into dough with rolling pin. Remove waxed paper.

Roll up rectangle, beginning at long side. Cut into 10 slices. Make 2 cuts in rounded side of each slice, ½ inch apart and ¾ of the way through slice.

Place on ungreased baking sheet; gently spread slices until they resemble fans. Cover; let rise in warm place until double, 45 to 60 minutes. (Dough is ready if an indentation remains when touched.)

Heat oven to 400°. Bake until rolls are deep golden brown, 10 to 12 minutes.

10 rolls.

Cream Buns

¼ cup sugar
3 tablespoons flour
¼ teaspoon salt
1 cup milk
2 egg yolks
1 teaspoon vanilla
½ Danish Pastry Dough (page 58), chilled

Mix sugar, flour and salt in saucepan. Stir in milk. Heat to boiling, stirring constantly. Boil and stir 1 minute. Remove from heat. Gradually stir half of the hot mixture into egg yolks. Stir into remaining hot mixture in pan. Heat just to boiling. Cool. Stir in vanilla. Refrigerate until stiff.

Roll dough into 12-inch square on lightly floured surface. Cut into nine 4-inch squares. Place ½ inch apart on ungreased baking sheet. Brush each square lightly with water.

Place 1 tablespoon chilled filling in center of each square. Fold 4 corners to center, securing by pressing down firmly in center.

Cover; let rise in warm place until double, about 45 minutes. (Dough is ready if an indentation remains when touched.)

Heat oven to 400°. Bake until rolls are deep golden brown, 10 to 12 minutes.

9 rolls.

Note: For variety, ½ recipe Prune-Apricot Filling (page 52) may be substituted for the cream filling in this recipe.

Bear Claws

½ Danish Pastry Dough (page 58), chilled
3 tablespoons currant jelly
3 tablespoons sliced almonds
1 egg white
1 teaspoon water
2 tablespoons sugar

Roll dough into 12-inch square on lightly floured surface. Cut into nine 4-inch squares. Spread 1 teaspoon jelly and 1 teaspoon almonds along center third of each square. Fold one side over to center; fold opposite side ½ inch over center and press gently to seal.

Turn pastries seam sides down. Make 4 cuts along one folded edge of each to within ½ inch of opposite folded edge. Place on ungreased baking sheet. Separate cuts to resemble bear claws.

Beat egg white and water slightly; brush over pastries. Sprinkle with sugar. Cover; let rise in warm place until double, 45 to 60 minutes. (Dough is ready if an indentation remains when touched.)

Heat oven to 400°. Bake until rolls are golden brown, 10 to 12 minutes.

9 rolls.

Italian Easter Bread

The Portuguese place one Easter egg in their traditional holiday bread; our modern Italian version has half a dozen! Have fun coloring the eggs first, or nestle them plain in this festive twist of lemony dough.

 2 packages active dry yeast
½ cup warm water (105 to 115°)
½ cup lukewarm milk (scalded, then cooled)
½ cup sugar
½ cup shortening
 1 teaspoon salt
 2 eggs
   Grated peel of 2 lemons (about 2 tablespoons)
4½ to 5 cups all-purpose* or unbleached flour
12 uncooked eggs (see note)
 1 egg yolk
 1 tablespoon water
   Tiny multicolored decorators' candies

Dissolve yeast in warm water in large mixing bowl. Stir in milk, sugar, shortening, salt, 2 eggs, the lemon peel and 2 cups of the flour. Beat until smooth. Mix in enough remaining flour to make dough easy to handle.

Turn dough onto lightly floured surface; knead until smooth and elastic. Place in greased bowl; turn greased side up. Cover; let rise in warm place until double, about 1½ hours. (Dough is ready if an indentation remains when touched.)

Punch down dough; let rise until almost double, about 30 minutes. Divide dough into 4 equal parts. Roll each part into a rope 36 inches long.

Place 2 ropes side by side on greased baking sheet; twist gently and loosely and shape into ring. Pinch ends to fasten. Twist remaining 2 ropes into another ring. Let rise until double, about 40 minutes.

Heat oven to 350°. Insert 6 eggs between ropes in each ring. Do not let eggs touch baking sheet; if they do, they will turn brown in that spot. Beat 1 egg yolk and 1 tablespoon water slightly; brush over bread. Sprinkle with candies.

Bake until bread is brown, about 25 minutes. Allow 1 egg for each serving. Store leftover bread in refrigerator.

2 rings (6 servings each).

*Do not use self-rising flour in this recipe.

Note: Color eggs if you wish. Mix 2 cups cold water, 1 teaspoon vinegar and ¼ teaspoon food color. Place eggs in mixture 30 minutes. Drain; let stand until completely dry.

Hot Cross Buns

2 packages active dry yeast
½ cup warm water (105 to 115°)
½ cup lukewarm milk (scalded, then cooled)
¾ cup unseasoned lukewarm mashed potatoes
½ cup sugar
1¼ teaspoons salt
½ cup butter or margarine, softened
2 eggs
1 teaspoon cinnamon
¼ teaspoon nutmeg
1 cup raisins
½ cup chopped citron
About 4½ cups all-purpose* or unbleached flour
1 egg yolk
2 tablespoons cold water
Quick White Icing (right)

Dissolve yeast in warm water in large mixing bowl. Stir in milk, potatoes, sugar, salt, butter, 2 eggs, the cinnamon, nutmeg, raisins, citron and 2 cups of the flour. Beat until smooth. Stir in enough remaining flour to make a soft dough.

Turn dough onto lightly floured surface; knead until smooth and elastic, about 5 minutes. Place in greased bowl; turn greased side up. Cover; let rise in warm place until double, about 1½ hours. (Dough is ready if an indentation remains when touched.)

Punch down dough; divide into fourths. Divide each fourth into 8 equal parts. Shape each part into a smooth ball, tucking edge under so it resembles a mushroom cap. Place about 2 inches apart on greased baking sheet or in 2 greased round layer pans, 9x1½ inches. With scissors, snip a cross in top of each ball. Let rise until double, about 40 minutes.

Heat oven to 375°. Beat egg yolk and cold water slightly; brush over tops of buns. Bake until buns are golden brown, about 20 minutes. Cool slightly; frost crosses with Quick White Icing.

32 buns.

*If using self-rising flour, omit salt.

Quick White Icing
Mix 1 cup confectioners' sugar, 1 tablespoon water or milk and ½ teaspoon vanilla until smooth.

What To Do If . . .

Dough doesn't rise? Too much heat may have "shocked" the yeast, or too little slowed it down. Check water temperature with a thermometer and keep rising dough covered and in a warm place out of drafts.

Dough rises too high? Dough has risen too long or at too high a temperature. Never set dough to rise in a heated oven or in direct sunlight. A temperature of 80 to 85° is just right.

Bread has big air holes? Next time firmly punch down dough and press or roll out gas bubbles.

Kugelhupf

While cakelike Kugelhupf is Viennese in origin, all Europeans share a similar Christmas sweet bread baked in a festive mold. Our modern mixer-easy recipe makes for year round dessert-and-coffee enjoyment.

1 package active dry yeast
¼ cup warm water (105 to 115°)
½ cup lukewarm milk (scalded, then cooled)
½ cup sugar
½ cup butter or margarine, softened
½ teaspoon salt
3 eggs
2¾ cups all-purpose* or unbleached flour
½ cup golden raisins
Grated peel of 1 lemon
⅓ cup very finely chopped almonds or dry bread crumbs
12 to 16 blanched almonds

Dissolve yeast in warm water in large mixer bowl. Add milk, sugar, butter, salt, eggs and 1¼ cups of the flour. Blend ½ minute on low speed, scraping bowl constantly. Beat 4 minutes on medium speed, scraping bowl occasionally.

Stir in raisins, lemon peel and remaining flour. Scrape batter from side of bowl. Cover; let rise in warm place until double, about 1½ hours. (Batter is ready if an indentation remains when touched.)

Grease side and bottom of bundt pan or 9-cup anodized aluminum ring mold; sprinkle with chopped almonds. Arrange blanched almonds evenly in bottom of pan. Stir down batter by beating about 25 strokes. Spoon batter evenly into pan. Let rise until double, about 1 hour.

Heat oven to 350°. Bake 50 minutes. Immediately remove from pan. (Pictured on page 65.)

1 loaf.

*Do not use self-rising flour in this recipe.

Bake a Holiday Gift

Few presents express your caring more than the ones you make yourself. And what better time to bake a gift than at Christmas or Easter, when nostalgia runs deep and you have the wealth of the world's holiday breads to choose from. Consider simply wrapping your gift in foil or plastic wrap and decorating with ribbon. Or pick out an attractive serving plate, tray or basket to hold what you've baked and gift wrap them together.

Pictured on page 65: Clockwise from upper left — Kugelhupf (page 64), Orange Pinwheels (page 49), Honey-Wheat Twist (page 53).

Pictured on page 66: Stollen (page 67).

Stollen

1 package active dry yeast
¾ cup warm water (105 to 115°)
½ cup sugar
½ teaspoon salt
3 eggs
1 egg, separated
½ cup butter or margarine, softened
3½ cups all-purpose* or
    unbleached flour
½ cup chopped blanched almonds
¼ cup cut-up citron
¼ cup cut-up candied cherries
    (optional)
¼ cup raisins
1 tablespoon grated lemon peel
¼ cup butter or margarine, softened
1 tablespoon water
    Confectioners' sugar or
    White Icing (right)
    Blanched almond halves
    Pieces of citron
    Candied cherry halves

Dissolve yeast in warm water in large mixer bowl. Add sugar, salt, 3 eggs, the egg yolk, ½ cup butter and 1¼ cups of the flour. Beat 10 minutes on medium speed, scraping bowl frequently.

Stir in remaining flour, ½ cup almonds, ¼ cup citron, ¼ cup cherries, the raisins and the lemon peel. Scrape batter from side of bowl. Cover; let rise in warm place until double, about 1½ hours.

Stir down batter by beating 25 strokes. Cover tightly; refrigerate 8 hours.

Turn batter onto well-floured surface; turn to coat with flour. Divide in half. Press each half into an oval, about 10x7 inches. Spread each oval with 2 tablespoons of the butter. Fold lengthwise in half; press only folded edge firmly.

Place stollen on greased baking sheet. Beat egg white and 1 tablespoon water slightly; brush over tops. Let rise until double, 45 to 60 minutes.

Heat oven to 375°. Bake until stollen are golden brown, 20 to 25 minutes. While warm, dust tops with confectioners' sugar or frost with White Icing. If desired, decorate with almond halves, pieces of citron and cherry halves to resemble poinsettias. (Pictured on page 66.)

2 stollen.

*Do not use self-rising flour in this recipe.

White Icing
Mix 1½ cups confectioners' sugar and 1½ tablespoons milk until smooth.

Panettone

2 packages active dry yeast
½ cup warm water (105 to 115°)
½ cup lukewarm milk (scalded, then cooled)
½ cup sugar
1 teaspoon salt
3 eggs
½ cup butter or margarine, softened
5 to 5½ cups all-purpose* or unbleached flour
½ cup golden raisins
½ cup chopped citron
2 tablespoons pine nuts (optional)
1 tablespoon anise seed
1 egg
1 tablespoon water

Dissolve yeast in warm water in large mixing bowl. Stir in milk, sugar, salt, 3 eggs, the butter and 2½ cups of the flour. Beat until smooth. Stir in raisins, citron, pine nuts, anise seed and enough remaining flour to make dough easy to handle.

Turn dough onto lightly floured surface; knead until smooth and elastic, about 5 minutes. Place in greased bowl; turn greased side up. Cover; let rise in warm place until double, 1½ to 2 hours. (Dough is ready if an indentation remains when touched.)

Punch down dough; divide in half. Shape each half into a round, slightly flat loaf. Place loaves in opposite corners of greased baking sheet. Cut a cross ½ inch deep on top of each loaf. Let rise until double, about 1 hour.

Heat oven to 350°. Beat 1 egg and 1 tablespoon water slightly; brush over loaves. Bake until loaves are golden brown, 35 to 45 minutes.

2 loaves.

*If using self-rising flour, omit salt.

About Bread Baking

What do you have to know to bake your very first loaf of bread? What are some tips that can give a boost to even the most experienced baker? It's all gathered in this section: the background information, knowing tips, and step-by-step photographs that tell all about yeast baking.

About Bread Baking

What Is Bread Made Of?

Whether you're new to bread baking or about to graduate from simple to spectacular, take comfort in this: all yeast bakings, even the most exotic, share the same basic ingredients.

Flour: Most widely used is all-purpose enriched. This flour contains a special protein called gluten. When mixed with liquid and kneaded or beaten, the gluten in flour stretches like elastic, trapping the bubbles of gas formed by the yeast and building the structure of the bread. Since flours like cracked wheat, rye and soy lack sufficient gluten of their own, in bread recipes they are usually combined with all-purpose flour.

Self-rising flour, which already contains leavening and salt, is not often recommended for yeast breads. However, all of the recipes in this book have been tested with self-rising flour, and where it can be used, a note is included giving the adjustments you'll need to make.

Yeast: Yeast is a live plant which gives off a gas that makes dough rise. It comes two ways: active dry or compressed cake. (One packet of dry equals one ³/₅-ounce cake.) Our recipes use the active dry. While some manufacturers' directions may call for blending dry undissolved yeast with flour, our recipes follow the traditional method of first dissolving the yeast in warm water.

Liquid: Water and milk are most commonly used; occasionally, fruit juices. Water gives bread an especially crispy crust; milk, a velvety texture and added nutrients.

Note: For dissolving active dry yeast, water should be 105 to 115°. Why so fussy? Because yeast is very sensitive. Too much heat will kill it, while cold will stunt its growth.

Sweetener: Sugar, honey and molasses "feed" yeast, add flavor, help brown crust.

Salt: A flavor-upper that also serves to control yeast's growth.

Fat: Added for tenderness and flavor. For a soft shiny top, brush just-baked loaves with butter or shortening.

To these basics are often added eggs for good taste and richness. Sour cream, cheese, herbs and other flavorings spark yeast bakings with character and variety.

How Is Bread Made?

Primarily, there are two kinds of bread—kneaded and batter.

Kneaded breads: Over the centuries, bread has been brought to life by the traditional rhythm of push-and-pull, fold-and-press known as kneading. The dough is worked until it's springy, blistered with tiny bubbles under the surface and satiny-smooth on top. Besides being good exercise, the minutes spent feeling the dough grow under your hands are usually considered the most pleasantly fulfilling part of bread baking.

After kneading, dough is shaped. If it is too elastic and springs back, let it rest 10 minutes, then shape. To cut, use a very sharp knife or kitchen scissors.

Batter breads: Because less flour is used and the dough is stickier, these breads are beaten with a mixer with the first addition of flour instead of being kneaded. They are generally not shaped, and when baked have a more open-grained texture. Fragrant and flavorful, batter breads can be enjoyed freshly baked or frozen as soon as cooled.

Storage Hints

Refrigerating: One of the joys of yeast baking is having a cache of fresh dough in the refrigerator, ready to shape and bake at short notice. Except for plain bread, it surely can be done! Simply cut off as much as you need the first time and refrigerate the rest (at 45° or below). Do note these storage time differences for unbaked dough:

* Made with milk
  and at least ¼ cup sugar—3 days
* Made with water only—5 days
* Our mashed potato recipe—5 days
  (page 50)

To prepare dough for refrigerating: Grease top well; cover with moistureproof wrap, then a damp cloth. Keep cloth damp.

When ready to bake: Shape dough and let rise until doubled (about 1½ to 2 hours).

To keep homemade breads fresh: Wrap or bag snugly and store in cool, dry place, but not the refrigerator; it stales quickly there.

Freezing: A good rule to follow is "Bake first, then freeze." Frozen, unbaked dough won't rise as high or bake up as tender.

To freeze bread: Cool completely. Slicing now will save thawing time later. Seal tightly in moistureproof vaporproof wrap or bag. Store up to 12 months.

To thaw: Let stand, *still wrapped*, at room temperature about 3 hours. If unwrapped, moisture collects. Pop frozen slices right into the toaster.

To freeze coffee cakes and rolls: Cool thoroughly but don't frost or decorate. Wrap tightly as for bread. Store up to 9 months.

To thaw: Let stand, still wrapped, at room temperature for 2 to 3 hours. Or heat, wrapped in foil, 20 to 25 minutes.

High Altitude Baking

The higher the altitude, the faster dough rises. To avoid a coarse-grained bread, compensate in one or both of the following ways:

* Allow a shorter rising time—*just* until dough has doubled.
* Cut back a little on yeast used—or punch down and let dough rise one more time than the recipe calls for.

The Well-Equipped Bread Baking Corner

Bread making, which began by "baking" pounded grain on a hot stone, still requires comparatively simple tools: mixing bowls, measuring cups and spoons, mixing spoon (electric mixer is nice, too), rubber scraper, rolling pin, thermometer, ruler, wire racks, pastry brush and the right size baking pans. For these, choose anodized aluminum or darkened metal. Add to this list, of course, an oven with an accurate thermostat or oven thermometer and a kitchen timer to signal when rising and baking need to be checked.

1. Check water temperature with a thermometer. If it is 105 to 115°, sprinkle on the granular yeast and stir until dissolved.

2. After the first addition of flour has been beaten in, the dough will be quite soft and will fall in "sheets" off the spoon.

3. The second addition of flour makes the dough stiff enough to knead. Add and mix in only enough so dough leaves side of bowl almost clean.

4. To knead, fold dough toward you. With heels of hands, push dough away with short rocking motions. Turn quarter turn; repeat.

5. When the dough is properly kneaded, it will feel elastic and the surface will appear smooth and blistered.

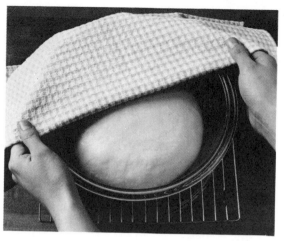

6. Dough should rise in a warm (80 to 85°) draft-free place. You may put bowl of dough on a wire rack over hot water and cover with a towel.

7. Dough should rise until double. Test by pressing fingertips ½ inch into dough. Impression will remain if dough has risen enough.

8. Punch center of dough down with your fist. Fold over and form into a ball. This releases large air bubbles to produce a finer texture.

9. To form a regular loaf of bread, flatten dough into a rectangle, 18x9 inches. Fold crosswise into thirds, overlapping the 2 ends.

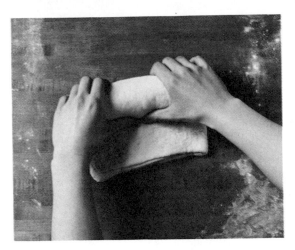

10. Roll dough tightly toward you, beginning at one of the open ends. Press with thumbs to seal after each turn. Pinch length of roll to seal.

11. With the side of your hand, press each end to seal; fold ends under. Place in a greased loaf pan to rise before baking.

12. Bake loaves with tops of pans in the middle of the oven. To test for doneness, tap crust with a wooden spoon: It should sound hollow.

Index